ARMED NON-STATE ACTORS IN INTERNATIONAL RELATIONS

A STUDY OF ISIS

ASHIM DHAKAL

Notion Press

Old No. 38, New No. 6
McNichols Road, Chetpet
Chennai - 600 031

First Published by Notion Press 2019
Copyright © Ashim Dhakal 2019
All Rights Reserved.

ISBN 978-1-68466-553-2

Contents

Acknowledgements

Firstly, I thank God Almighty for the blessings to complete this endeavor. A note of gratitude to a number of people whose genuine support and encouragement made this book a successful work. This book would not have been possible without the help of my supervisor Dr. Sebastian. N. His critical analysis helped this research to take the shape of what it is today. This book began and ended with the dedicated guidance and enormous help from him. I also express my sincere thanks to the faculty members of Sikkim University, Department of International Relations/Politics, Dr. Manish and Ph Newton for their valuable advises. It was indeed their constant support, encouragement and patience, which contributed at the large in the process of this research. I would also like to express my gratitude to my family for giving me moral support and encouragement, which helped me to proceed with my work.

I thank you all once again, and would like to sincerely admit that my work would not have been what it is today, without your support.

– **Ashim Dhakal**

Introduction

This book provides an elucidation on the role of the Armed Non-State Actors in International Relations through an analysis of ISIS. This study has examined the evolutionary and defining characteristics of Armed Non-State Actors (ANSAs) and introduced a framework based on their autonomy, representation and influence (ARI). This study also provides an analysis of ascent, mobilisation strategy and impact of ISIS in international relations and how it is unfathomably co-related with ANSAs. Some of the major questions addressed in this study are: How political instability in West Asia triggered the growth of ISIS as an ANSA? What is the modus operandi/mobilisation strategy of ISIS? What has been the impact of ISIS in IR?

In the study of international relations (IR), states had traditionally been the centre of the discourse; such state-centric elucidation concentrates on a Westphalian model of the nation-state that laid down the foundation of contemporary state system and understanding of international relations. Theoretically, the understanding of IR was dominated by realist paradigms and the field, often described as the child of Morgenthau, Hobbesian, Machiavellian etc. revolved around the concept of power. However, the end of bipolarity witnessed a paradigm shift in IR where states were not able to provide elucidation on the power shift that was taking place, and various players had emerged in the realm of international relations.

The end of the Cold War witnessed a power shift in two distinct ways. The first is in a geographical sense with power moving from certain traditional strong states such as U.K and U.S to other states like China and Japan. The second is parallel where power is shifting from State to Non-State Actors (NSAs). Parallel Shift is more transformative and is substantially a different kind of shift (Aydinli, 2016). In such circumstances, new actors have increased their involvement in IR. Scholarly analysis in the discourse was built on state, not NSAs. There is a less comprehensive understanding of o NSAs. If one agrees on parallel shift, then such transformation needs further theoretical analysis. Theories like functionalism, Neo-functionalism, Liberalism et al. does incorporate NSAs role. But the importance of NSAs remains heavily entangled in various assumptions and analysis. These problems need to be addressed from an IR perspective.

There is an intricacy in defining NSAs in a predicament where the understanding is entangled in various analyses and understanding. State and NSAs are divergent but analysing NSA independently without the state would be misleading. State, on one hand, supports private banks, INGOs, MNC and also receives help from such NSAs. On the other hand, there are groups that are seen as threats by the states. Such NSAs include cross-border radical groups, terrorists etc. There are autonomous NSAs that function without the state's support such as armed groups, human trafficking, drug mafia etc. On the other hand, there are semi-autonomous NSAs that are supported by a state such as banks, NGOs etc. (Wallace and Josselin, 2001). Such confusions have to be disentangled in order to understand the role played by NSAs. To circumvent such confusions, the definition of NSAs itself has to be reiterated.

Clear concepts have not yet been tracked in defining NSAs. The understanding of NSAs attracts intricacy where various scholars have opposing views in defining NSAs. Huntington defined Clash of Civilisations as NSAs. Biersteker's understanding was based on types of authority, and William Wallace and Josselin defined NSAs based on transnationalism (Aydinli, 2016). There are various frameworks laid down in understanding NSAs. Some of these look at the capacity of implementing policy and decision, shared interest, values, principles, shared norms, goals, autonomy etc. This understanding gives a framework for the analysis of NSAs. However, the problem still lies in defining violent groups, terror threats, organised crime etc. Similarly, there is also a struggle to explain why influential countries like U.S, U.K, France, Britain, Russia etc. have to concern themselves with the weak, failing states (Fidler, 2008) that become breeding grounds for Armed NSAs threatening their existence itself. The framework in which NSA has been laid doesn't explain these emerging threats.

Researchers have often been biased in understanding NSA's threat. They tend to overlook the threat posed by various armed groups. This happens when they are theorised by liberal understanding and focuses more on NGOs etc. Another possible reason for overlooking NSA's threat is because they consider them as a part of terrorist studies, studies on organised crime etc. It was only after the 9/11 attacks that more work appeared on NSA's threat, but it was very limited. Works on NSA's threat includes transnational criminal activity, organised violence, terrorism etc. Researchers in that manner further conceptualised NSA's threat, and the concept moved along with a spectrum from relatively more statist to more non-statist. In such a framework, scholars like Oliver Roy, Steve Call et al. conceptualised NSA's threat in a much broader sense of Armed Non-State Actors (ANSA) providing deeper insights and evolution of ANSAs (Aydinli, 2016).

It is clear that the term Armed Non-State Actors (ANSA) was born because of the complexity of NSAs in defining itself. When NSAs uses radical means or arms, then it is referred to as Armed Non-State Actors (ANSA). There is no universally agreed definition of ANSAs. However, the term is used to indicate organised armed entities that are primarily motivated by political goals, operate outside effective state control, and lack legal capacity to become a party to relevant international treaties. This includes Non-State Armed Groups, national liberation movements, de-facto governing authorities and states that are not or only partially recognised. ANSAs are usually engaged in armed struggle against state forces or other ANSAs in the context of non-international armed conflict or other situations of violence. ANSAs have emerged in a substantial part because of the growing infirmity of many states that they seek to perpetuate and intensify (Ataman, 2003). ANSAs are also an extensive area; its dynamic can be understood by using autonomy, representation, influence (ARI) framework.

In the post 9/11 era, the understanding of ANSAs has been revolutionised with the emergence of ISIS as part of the latest phase of ANSAs. This transformation has severe political and theoretical implications for IR and must be given further analysis. Their modus operandi has transformed the understanding into perilous ANSAs and evolution with ANSAs. Their actions and influence have to be counted as the evidence of evolving ANSAs that need further analysis under the framework of ANSAs. Analysing ISIS independently without considering its radical ideological base would be meaningless. Similarly, it has to be looked from the prism of ANSAs in order to understand the wider implications for IR discourse.

ISIS as the focus of my study, its ideological awakening lie in the radical interpretation of Islam by

Ibn Tamiyyad, Sayid Qutb, Al-Afghani, Mohammed Abduh, Osama Bin Laden, Abu Mus'ab al-Suri's, Ayatollah Ruhollah Khomeini, Abdul A'al Mawdudi, Abu Muhammed al-Maqdisi et al. However, its organisational foundation has a long evolving period following the toppling of Saddam Hussein to the rise of Abu Musab al Zarqawi in Iraq. It was from 2002–2006 that Zarqawi built his forces in Iraq. Initially, it was Tawid Wal-Jihad, and later it turned into Al-Qaeda in Iraq (AQI) after pledging bayat[1] with Bin Laden's Al-Qaeda. Zarqawi took advantage of the Sunni antagonism towards U.S forces and the sentiment of Sunni disenfranchisement at the hands of Kurds and Shiites to carry out inimitable sectarian agenda that dwarfed Al-Qaeda in assorted ways. After the death of Zarqawi at the hands of U.S forces in June 2006, AQI merged with jihadist insurgents Mujahedeen Shura Council and announced the formation of Islamic State of Iraq (ISI) under the leadership of Omar Al-Baghdadi (Hosken, 2015). However, in 2010, ISI lost Omar Al-Baghdadi. At that time it was believed that ISI was weakened, but not eliminated. It was in 2011 after U.S withdrawal that ISI regained its strength under the leadership of Ibrahim al-Badri al Samarra'I (Abu Bakr Al-Baghdadi).

When Abu Bakr Al-Baghdadi took over ISI, another significant event engulfed the region. Radical Islamic

---

1   Bayat in Islamic terminology is an oath of allegiance.

Fundamentalism politics epitomised by ANSAs such as Al-Qaeda was represented in wider ways. The Arab Awakening[2] witnessed the political transformation in North Africa and West Asia. In countries like Egypt, Yemen, Libya and Tunisia there was political transformation and attempted political insurrection was seen in Bahrain and Syria.

In part, this transition and the role of ANSAs were seen across the region. In Syria, Assad used force to suppress the uprising demanding freedom. In Iraq, Maliki was using aggressive policies to suppress the Sunnis and marginalised them. The outcome of these policies in Iraq and Syria took off disastrously. Abu Bakr Al-Baghdadi united the marginalised Sunni population from Iraq and strengthened his foothold. At the same time there was a formation of an armed group in Syria named Al-Nusra under Jawlini. Al-Nusra was fighting against the hostile policies of Assad in Syria (Stern and Berger, 2015). It was in this situation that ISI emerged as powerful ANSAs after merging with Al-Nusra. The new group was known as the Islamic State of Iraq and Levant (ISIL/ISIS) in 2013. However, Al-Nusra did not accept this merger, but still, ISIS carried out its atrocities independently.

---

2   Commonly referred as Arab Spring or Arab Uprising, it was a wave of change In North Africa and West Asia where people were revolting against authoritarian regimes for freedom and economic justice.

Like an avenging fire, ISIS growled east across the border from Syria into Iraq. The rampant expansion of ISIS as ANSAs gained the glare of publicity in the international arena. ISIS claimed to establish an Islamic State and called out to Muslims all across the world for *Hijrah*[3] and fight against the *takfirs*[4] and join to help ISIS for *Global Jihad*[5]. This sent a wave of fear among the countries in West Asia and Western countries. ISIS as an armed no – state actor came to the spotlight and a new threat perception was seen across the globe that came from ANSAs and not states. In Iraq, ISIS had taken control over Tikrit, Baiji, Qaim, Rutba, Anah, Ramadi, Falluja, Tal Afar, Haditha Dam, Mosul, Samarra, Anbar, Kirkuk, Erbil and other territories. In Syria, ISIS took control over the cities held by Al-Nusra and other rebel groups as war within war emerged. Initially, when the situation was ripe for ISIS to expand, they took Dier Al Zour and later, ISIS took the cities of Raqqa, Aleppo, Hama, Homs, Palmyra and other Sunni villages in

---

3   Emigration; the path of the Prophet Mohammed from Mecca to Medina to find Islam in 622; Used by ISIS to signify abandoning past lives and move to ISIS controlled territory or mentally departing from family/friends/Muslims to carry out atrocities without their knowledge.

4   Non believer.

5   Being prepared to lay down their lives to what they see as service of Allah is Jihad. Global Jihad is a created terminology which means that Muslims all across the globe should give their life in service of Allah. Today, ISIS is using Global Jihad as their recruitment strategy.

the region. With this it was clear that ISIS has taken over massive amounts of land in Iraq and Syria which had become a concern for the west as it challenges their interest in the region. ISIS emerged as a potent Armed Non-State Actor in West Asia occupying a landmass as big as the United Kingdom.

ISIS in its self-proclaimed caliph seeks to establish Islamic State and have claimed certain portions across the world starting from its de-facto region of Iraq and Syria in West Asia. ISIS claims the region of Africa; in Western Africa they claimed certain regions under Islamic State mandate and called it Maghreb, in Northern Africa Land of Alkinana, Central and Western Africa Land of Habasha. In West Asia it claims over all the countries and names as Hijaz, Yaman, Sham and Iraq. ISIS has claimed the region in Europe which includes Portugal and Spain; Andalus, some portions of France and the former Yugoslavia; Oroba. Turkey; Anatol. Afghanistan and Pakistan; Kordistan and the region in India, Central Asia and West China calling it Land of Khurasan; areas under the influence of ISIS has expanded over the years. From pledging Bayats to recruitment, ISIS has dwarfed other Armed Non-State Actors in this regard.

ISIS brought about a very different form of terrorism by metamorphosing radical Islamic fundamentalism and redefining security in IR which was not done by the previous organisations giving a wider connotation to understanding ANSAs. They aim to maintain *Ummah*[6] for Sunni Muslims and achieve their dream of establishing the caliphate. ISIS has been recruiting fighters via online platforms like Twitter by creating 50,000[7] Twitter accounts and various other sources. The fighters join the organisation from all over the world. ISIS has become a global ANSA recruiting 70,000[8] fighters including 15,000–20,000[9] foreign fighters who are employed to strike different countries.

ISIS is now the principal opponent of western countries. ISIS is accused of generating a massive humanitarian crisis in the region. From their bombing tactics to beheading and lone wolf attacks, ISIS is said to be one of the most radical ANSAs in history, dwarfing Al-Qaeda. Also, ISIS is said to be the richest ANSA in the world where it has commandeered eleven oil fields (Johny, 2015) in Syria and Iraq which have the capacity to produce 75,000 barrels a day (ibid). ISIS is rewriting the rules of Islamic Extremism and Fundamentalism using sophisticated techniques of distribution and manipulation, where more jihads are joining the organisation. It is not a change but an evolution and their new ideas and practices are sending shock waves around

6   The worldwide community of Muslims is known as Ummah. In political Islam, it means a common brotherhood.

7   See, *Economist*. 2015. Islamic State: The propaganda war. August 15, pp 41-42.

8   ibid.

9   ibid.

the world. They have seized sophisticated weapons and war machines from the captured territories; their methodology of waging an attack is different compared to traditional terrorist groups. They are highly intellectual and are referred to as intellectual terrorists.

The rise of ISIS has now become a global concern. Countries are now involved either directly or indirectly to brawl this armed Non-State Actor. Countries like Russia, The United States of America and France are active in the region and West Asian countries like Saudi Arabia, Iran, Iraq, Syria, Turkey are heavily involved in this crisis. Since WWII this is the first time that a coalition is formed to combat ANSAs. However, there is an ambiguity in solving the crisis because the countries have their own curiosity. U.S and Russia are traditional rivals and have always been in resolving the conflict. Regional bipolar antagonism between Iran and Saudi Arabia also exists for solving this issue. Countries like France, Syria and other countries as well as groups like FSA etc. have their own interest. It can be said that the conflict in the region is not going to end in the near future. Currently there is a tug of war in Mosul between ISIS rebels and Iraqi forces assisted by the United States. Similar is the case in Aleppo, where Vladimir Putin and Assad are on one side and rebels on the other side. Recently there was a chemical attack at Khan Sheikhoun in Syria and U.S responded to this attack by using Tomahawk Missiles at Shayrat Airfield in Syria is a clear indication that the conflict is not going to end soon. Such antagonism among various countries solving the Syrian issue will add further impairment to the crisis.

In this context, the United Nations Security Council (UNSC) has adopted a resolution to strengthen international judicial cooperation in countering ANSAs like ISIS. Resolution 2322 looks to improve the effectiveness of International Legal and Judicial systems in their fight against terrorism. Countries have been actively meddling in West Asia to brawl the issue of ISIS.

Islamic Fundamentalism since 1945; written by Beverley Milton Edwards (2005) looks at the foundation of Islamic fundamentalism and the effects of colonialism in the Islamic world. The book sheds light on the expansion of Islamic fundamentalism, focusing on events like the 1979 Iranian Revolution and the emergence of Al-Qaeda, Hezbollah and others. It further analyses how these actors are driven by their fundamentalist approach. The book provides a reliable account of the causes and the diversity of Islamic fundamentalism which is a modern-day phenomenon. It explains how Islamic fundamentalism has grabbed the headlines posing a grave threat to the West which has become a potentially revolutionary trend in West Asia. *Empire of Fear* by Andrew Hosken (2015) delivers the inside story of Islamic State. Through extensive first-hand reporting, he builds a comprehensive picture of IS, their brutal ideology and exterminationist methods. This masterpiece reveals how IS came to be, explores their goals and asks how they can be defeated.

ISIS the State of Terror written by Jessica Stern and J.M Berger (2015) explains the evolution of ISIS from Iraq invasion to Arab Spring and the present day. It explains how ISIS evolved during these events that led to the growth of the fundamentalist approach and the implications of ISIS in West Asia and beyond. It also focuses on their access to intelligence sources like online recruiting, psychological factors which attracts people to join the organisation, the state under ISIS, humanitarian crisis and genocide. William Wallace and Daphne Josselin in the book *Non-State Actors in World Politics* (2001), discusses a diverse range of economic, social, legal and illegal Non-State Actors such as Catholic Church, trade unions, Diasporas, religious movements, transnational corporation and organised crime. They analyse how the involvement of Non-State Actors in world politics has evolved over a period of time. The book raises important questions such as the sources of influence, strategies, and targets of Non-State Actors. This book throws open a debate on whether Non-State Actors should be considered autonomous from the states or not.

In 2014, Islamic State seemingly appeared out of nowhere conquering Mosul, Iraq's second largest city and boldly announcing the establishment of a caliphate that seeks to eliminate borders of West Asia and expand further to India, Central Asia, former Yugoslavia and other parts of Europe. Today, it controls thousands of square miles. Charles R. Lister in his book *the Islamic State* which is forwarded by Ahmed Rashid (2015) traces the outfit's growth of Abu Musab Al-Zarqawi to its stunning maturation in Iraq and Syria. He helps scholars understand what to expect next and recommends actions to defeat the group.

Violent Non-State Actors: From Anarchist to Jihadist written by Ersel Aydinli (2016), examines the defining characteristics and evolutionary dynamics of VNSAs and introduces a framework based on their autonomy, influence and representation providing a comparative analysis of the late 19th and early 20th century's anarchist movement and present-day jihadist networks. It explores the distinct characteristics of the anarchist and jihadist as VNSA with global potential, not just describing them but also seeking to understand what they are instances of. This book considers the types of changes that have occurred in the last 150 years and the possible role VNSA may play in future. This book provides further theoretical implications for the study of NSA and transnational actors.

Coalition Contribution in Countering Islamic State: A Report by Congressional Research Service (2016), analyses how a global coalition is formed to counter Islamic State. It further provides thinking ground for military aspect of coalition such as NATO, Russia, Turkey and others role in combating ISIS and the challenges to coalition coherence. The report by the United Nations Security Council on their 7272 meeting had an agenda on the issue of threat to international peace and security caused by terrorist acts (2014). This agenda dealt with terrorist threats in international peace and included presidents and representatives from U.S, Argentina, U.K, Chad Chile, China, France, Jordan, Lithuania, Luxembourg, Nigeria, Republic of Korea and Russia.

An Analysis of Abu Mus'ab al-Suri's "Call to Global Islamic Resistance" written by M.W Zackie Masoud (2013) analyses text written by Suri who was a key architect post 9/11 attacks. Masoud in this article explains the text of Suri's "Call to Global Islamic Resistance." Suri's text has now become a template for jihad and is also considered as Mein Kampf of the jihadist movement. The domination by western consumerism and its effect on Muslims is well explained in this article. The text by Suri invites readers to self-recruit and become independent terrorists. Masoud in this article explains how Suri's text has invited or magnetised support for jihadist movements across the globe.

ISIS Global Messaging Strategy Factsheet written by Jessica Lewis McFate and Harleen Gambhir (2014) brings forth the psychological factors that have added to the ISIS foothold. It further provides explanations on how 'lone wolf attacks,' alliances and recruitment process have expanded over a period of time and what are the factors that have led to ISIS's strategic success.

The *Islamic State Origin Goals and Future Implications* by Colin Tucker (2014), explicates methodology, resource distribution, success, relationships, structure, financial base armaments et al of Islamic State and shows further implications on how would the situation in the region be with ISIS become as a strong actor and what would be the social implication on Sunni and Shia's Muslims is covered in this article.

Islamic State of Iraq and Syria: A threat to Global Peace and Security written by Justina Alaneme and Canon Egesi (2015), provides a brief history of some of the radical Islamic groups such as Hezbollah, Hamas, Al-Qaeda et al and provides discussion on the rise of ISIS and how it has changed the threat perception in global politics.

Rise of Islamic Caliphate Impacting West Asia's Stability authored by Gurmeet Kanwal (2014) explains how West Asia has been a volatile region where numerous conflicts have occurred and in this scenario instability in Iraq and Syria led to the growth of ISIS. It throws argument on ISIS and its impact on the West Asian region.

Conventional IR theories have paid scant attention to NSA/ANSAs threats. ANSA is an endemic feature of IR and pose a wide array of threats in IR. They challenge state legitimacy through violent actions and threaten greater regional instability. These actions fall directly into the realm under the non-traditional understanding of IR which academics and policy makers have been slow to understand and analyse. Overlapping networked relationships, the decline of state-centric comprehension of IR and the rise of more globalised environments have created a more accommodating system for ANSAs. ANSAs have emerged in a substantial part because of the growing infirmity of many states that they seek to perpetuate and intensify.

The best way to understand contemporary states is in terms of strong-weak gamut across certain key dimensions such as; legitimacy, capacity, collective interest, individual interest etc. when these dimensions along which the state is weak, the prospects for the rise of ANSA are considerably increased. In a similar situation ANSAs have expanded across the globe. ISIS came into being because of the failure of the state in key dimensions like legitimacy, capacity, collective interest, individual interest etc. Several other ANSAs have also emerged in similar situations which was visualised during the Arab Awakening and these groups operating in other parts of the world have pledged alliance with ISIS strengthening the extensiveness of ISIS and expanding ANSAs in world politics. These developments need further analysis from an IR perspective but such analysis lack in IR.

The manner in which we understand international relations is based on the Westphalian model of State-Centric Approach. Such an understanding laid the foundation of IR. However, the end of the Cold War witnessed a new shift in the field where threat perception has changed from state to Armed Non-State Actors. In this regard, this study uses ISIS as a case to understand the wider implications of ANSAs in IR. This study provides an understanding of changes that have been taking place in IR specifically focusing on ISIS as an armed

Non-State Actor. This study further produces an explanatory framework on modus operandi of ISIS and how ISIS is using nucleus concept of radical Islamic fundamentalism as their ideological base to carry out their political and religious operations in West Asia and beyond. Keeping in mind the above discussions and lacuna, the researcher tries to: 1: Examine the emergence of ISIS as a prominent Armed Non-State Actors (ANSA).2: Analyse the ideology, organisation and structure of ISIS.

To comprehend the magnitude of Armed Non-State Actors and its expansion, researchers have used the Theory of Open Source Anarchy. The Theory of Open Source Anarchy (OSA) was developed by David P. Fidler (2008) to understand the shift that is taking place in the 21st century. The theory explains how NSA/ANSA use independent material power that not only challenges state but also transforms anarchy that continues to epitomise state as superior. The theory throws light on how anarchy today reflects the ability of NSA/ANSAs to use material power in ways by affecting IR.

OSA attempts to communicate that the leading theories of IR do not adequately explain IR in the 21st century. OSA posit that anarchy has now become accessible to NSA/ANSAs as never before. This access has heavy implications for IR. The traditional theories in IR do not incorporate NSA/ANSAs in their study and they cannot explain violent actors, terror threats, organised crime et al. Similarly, they also struggle to explain why powerful countries like the U.S have to concern themselves with the weak, failing states that become breeding grounds for ANSAs threatening their existence itself. Ideas and material capabilities of NSA/ANSAs provide them with direct access to influence how anarchy operates. End of the Cold War, the emergence of the U.S. as a superpower and globalisation lowered the barriers for NSA/ANSAs to access over the condition of anarchy and changed the elasticity between power and ideas in IR (Fidler, 2008).

No better example of the growth and use of material power by ANSAs can be found on ISIS. ISIS repeated attack across the globe, alliances, online recruitments et al have dramatically affected foreign policy of other countries. ISIS has accessed anarchy and influenced its dynamics in ways that many states could never imagine accomplishing. ISIS also illustrates the elasticity of power and ideas in OSA. ISIS use of the internet for recruitment provides a potent example of how elasticity between power and ideas could be dangerous even for the world's most powerful states.

In keeping with the above-mentioned discussion, the following research questions are proposed:

1. How political instability in West Asia triggered the growth of ISIS as an ANSA?

2. What are the modus operandi/ mobilisation strategy of ISIS?

3. What has been the impact of ISIS in IR?

To comprehend the magnitude of Armed Non-State Actors in the post 9/11 era, this study has used secondary sources and available literature in this regard. A methodological aspect of the study is more inclined towards Qualitative method and available literature in this regard. The researcher has used secondary data collection – books, journals, newspapers, websites, archival documents, media etc. The researcher has further used the Historical Analytical Method to understand the scenario as constituted by other prominent actors in international relations and to draw out inferences to pertaining ANSAs and its co-relation with ISIS.

Introduction illustrates the main problems, delineates the main problems, and identifies the focal point of the research on the broader question of how NSAs emerged as a third eye and its materialisation into ANSAs. It will also give a brief account of the rise of ISIS as a contemporary issue in IR. It also gives prologue to research.

Chapter I focuses on the Historical and Theoretical perspective giving a comprehension of the state-centric approach in international relations and how international relations have transformed with an entry of armed non-sate actors (ANSA). It will provide a definition on ANSAs and identify typologies of ANSAs. This chapter further elucidates the role of ANSAs in IR and provides an understanding of the autonomy of ANSAs using an autonomy, representation and influence (ARI) framework.

Chapter II analyses the materialisation of ISIS as a powerful ANSAs and how they are diverse from other ANSAs. Examining the political instability in West Asian countries, this chapter scrutinises how ISIS came into being and the factors responsible for the rise and growth of ISIS. The researcher further elucidates the transformation of ISIS into a power ANSAs visioning their religious and political ideology.

Chapter III provides an understanding of modus operandi of ISIS. It makes the readers aware of how ISIS operates by providing an understanding of administration and hierarchy that formulates readers with the command structure of ISIS. It also provides an explanatory framework on recruitment strategy and policy of ISIS where thousands of fighters have joined ISIS to fight intruders in the region. Further, this chapter elucidates an understanding of financial networks of ISIS and weaponry.

Chapter IV diversifies the role of religion in IR by providing analysis of how region theorisation in IR is possible. Contemplating religion and IR, this section has built an analysis on the contemporary role of religion in IR with an analysis on ISIS and how it has shaped the whole security dilemma of IR post 9/11 period. The researcher has further explicated the attacks, violation of human rights etc. that ISIS has carried out leading to a massive humanitarian crisis and antagonism between West Asian countries, foreign powers skirmishing ISIS and future prospects.

The conclusion summarises the main argument of the chapters and attempts to provide an answer to various questions put forth. It also tries to provide an analysis of the problems and findings of the study.

Chapter 1

The Emergence of Armed Non-State Actors and Its Role in International Relations

1.1 Introduction

In the study of international relations (IR), states had traditionally been the centre of analysis; such state-centric elucidation concentrates on the Westphalian model of the nation-state that laid down the foundation of the contemporary international system and the study of international relations. Foundational background of IR can be traced by looking at historical events such as the Treaty of Westphalia, French Revolution, Congress of Vienna, WWI and WWII that shaped the understanding of IR from the state-centric approach. The IR academy was dominated and flooded by realist paradigms focusing on state entities only. However, after the 1970s, new thinking began to emerge that challenged the state-centric outlook and gave a new perspective to the discourse. Theories like Critical Theory, constructivism, feminism etc. brought in a new dynamic in the understanding of the discourse but the role played by Non-State entities remained entangled in various analysis and paradigms. The end of the Cold War brought in new players in the international arena where Non-State Actors (NSA) emerged as influential players in world politics. The dominant state-centric theories in IR do not incorporate such conversions and NSA's role into consideration.

This chapter attempts to bring in clarity in understanding NSAs from various theoretical perspectives and place the concept in a proper frame of reference. The chapter also discusses how the state-centric paradigm in IR evolved and the limitations it has. The changed IR also calls for rethinking of paradigms in IR to understand the role played by NSAs particularly where states have become vulnerable to newly emerging players in IR with the further materialisation of NSAs into ANSAs. Furthermore, this chapter will provide a foundation of analysis for NSAs and how there is an intricacy in defining NSAs and how we fit in ANSAs in IR and also their autonomy using an Autonomy Representation and Influence (ARI) framework of analysis.

1.2 State-Centric Paradigms in IR

All the conventional ideas and understandings of IR as a discipline date from early European consideration in the early modern days. The early version of principles of peaceful coexistence and system of sovereign states was established and invented at the Westphalian settlement of 1648. The Westphalian system emerged from the thirty years of war between the Catholics and the Protestants. Westphalia is also used to identify the state-centric characters of world order that premised on the full participation of members being accorded exclusively to territorially-based sovereign states (Falk, 2002).

Both history and the growth of thought encompass an understanding of the discourse where it took several years to develop a basic vocabulary of IR. The French Revolution for instance, its fateful ten years from 1789 to 1799 abolished monarchy and feudalism and the privileges of the churches. In short, it led to the rise of Napoleon Bonaparte and French Colonialism in Europe. From the religious fratricide of Westphalia and the French Revolution and its violent Napoleonic war to Congress of Vienna took into account the relationship of security and legitimacy and such long-established understandings laid the foundation of IR and practices in world politics.

All the conventional ideas of IR discipline date from the European side thought from the early modern period to post-medieval politics. Classical literature for instance, produced in combination the structure which continues to this day to frame most of the thinking in IR. The basic framework of classical thinking and literature was described with compelling lucidity producing a conceptual toolbox which continues, to this day, to dominate both the practice and interpretation of IR (Banks, 1984).

The classical literature was viewed as a single body of thought at the initial stage in IR. Both the historical, pre-modern work and also middle ages writings from 1648–1914 periods were used to develop an understanding and paradigm in IR. The itemise policy advise of Vishnu Gupta and Machiavelli, the wise historical observation of Thucydides, the moral forcefulness of the medieval just-war theorists, the soaring humanity of Kantian philosophy and the Hobbesian perspective of world defined by insecurity or the Clausewitzian strategic theory has produced a conceptual toolbox which continues to dominate both the practice and interpretation of IR. These classic works of literature endowed the world with an intellectual heritage richer by far that set the basic vocabulary of IR.

Outside the classical heritage, the world event further enriched the discourse with a set of ideas that went much farther (Banks, 1984). When the colossal ludicrousness of the First World War triggered, new thinking emerged and there was a burst of activity in universities. The First World War came to an end with the signing of the Treaty of Versailles. The U.S President Woodrow Wilson came up with fourteen points to strengthen peace and harmony in IR. On his 14th point he said that there would be a general association of nations to preserve peace. League of Nations was formed post-WWI in order to preserve peace and maintain stability in the world order.

After the Versailles settlement, there was a birth of new discourse associated with the world's first chair for the study of international politics where the Department of International Politics was created at the University College of Wales, Aberystwyth. At this time, an idealist wing of mainstream thinking came to dominate curricula. Classical rationalisations of great power rule of the world were abandoned to be replaced by collective security thinking, the idea of self-determination etc. which became practical strategies. Thus, liberal idealism emerged as a school of thought in IR.

Idealism is a doctrine which looks to transform the society and create a harmonious world order. This doctrine emphasised on the growing importance of interdependency and unity of mankind which could be brought about by the League of Nations. The Inter-War period of 1919–1939 was the theoretical field for idealists. In this period, countries followed the policy of isolation and war had been at a standstill. Nations indulged in building up their economies.

The disintegration of idealism was gesticulated after the publication of E.H Carr's *Twenty Years Crisis* in 1939. This work owed its impact not just to its critique of idealism but also changing of world events. There was economic depression; League of Nations had failed because of expansionist activities of Mussolini, Adolf Hitler and Tojo. The outbreak of World War II in 1939 helped to consolidate the realist position as an expansion of IR. Realism therefore denied itself against an idealist position and emerged as a dominant theory of IR after World War II and substantially laid the foundation of a state-centric outlook in IR.

Realism exercised a hegemonic position in IR for much of the twentieth century. The field of IR was often understood as a child of Hobbesian and Machiavellian that revolved around the concept of power. The understanding of IR was limited, and it was more concentrated on power and national interest. Conventional warfare and diplomacy were seen as the primary means by which states should protect themselves from the threat represented by armed forces.

A realist understanding of world politics considered the state as the sole and homogenous actor who occupied the mainstream IR as universal to explain state behaviour. The theoretical analysis of realist thinkers like Morgenthau, E.H Carr, Waltz, Mearsheimer et al. views the dynamics of world politics from the lenses of state behaviour (Brown and Ainley, 2005). For instance, Morgenthau believed that power is the ultimate aim of international politics (Robinson, 1969). Similarly, John Mearsheimer believes that great powers are the main actors of world politics (Mearsheimer, 2001). Scholars like Kenneth Waltz pointed out that all states in the international system are made functionally similar by constraints of the structure. The anarchic realm imposes a discipline on states: they are all required to pursue security before they can perform any other functions. Another leading scholar within the realist domain, Thomas Shelling pointed out that diplomacy is an intelligent use of power and described how to employ it intelligently (Scott, Richard et al, 2001)

Theoretically, it is lucid that the understanding of IR was dominated by state-centric outlook in many forms since the Treaty of Westphalia. States were considered as major actors in IR. From the idealist perspective to realist, neo-realist, neo-realist stability etc. IR was looked from a perspective of a state-centric approach. The state-centric framework has portrayed mankind as divided into separate sovereign state, each keeping law and order within its borders by application of force from the centre, and also using force to maintain security against other states. Relations between states were conducted by diplomacy against a background of military preparedness and alliances and within a limited code of International Law of which states, not people, were the subjects (Banks, 1979).

1.3 Challenges to State-Centric Paradigms in IR

The traditional understanding of IR has been challenged by many scholars because it privileges the state with an emphasis on power. This leads to the most fundamental signs of rethinking and call for broadening the understanding of IR. There were developments which the traditional state-centric theories in IR could not incorporate into their comprehension.

During the 1970s, IR became fragmented into a specialism and various paradigms. An understanding emerged that challenged the traditional understanding of IR because of its inability to understanding world politics. The discourse in IR has a long evolutional history, starting from the first debate (Traditionalism) to third debate (Post-Positivist/Reflexivity), IR has now become a mature discipline. It is clear that the initial stage of IR was more dominated by realist paradigm. As events unfolded in global politics, there were issues that were not looked upon by state-centric theories. Within such a myriad of state-centric outlook, various challenges emerged that changed the comprehension of IR in broader ways. Critical Theory, feminism, constructivism etc. changed the understanding and theorisation of IR.

The mainstream IR theories remain essentially conservative, connected with the maintenance of state power. From a theoretical perspective, Critical Theory exposes the historical structures of international power and develops knowledge that might contribute to the progressive and emancipatory transformation of world order. Borrowing ideas from Critical Theory, writers such as Robert Cox and Richard Ashley began to expose the theoretical domination of state-centric theories (Burchill, Devetak et al, 2005). The epistemological critiques of state-centric theories by Cox and Ashley expose the conservative ideology which underwrites the theoretical approach. Both Ashley and Cox highlight the extent to which state-centric theories naturalise or reify the international system by treating structures which have a specific and transitory history as if they were permanent given figures (ibid). Robert Cox succinctly and famously said that theory is for someone and for some purpose (ibid), to criticise state-centric paradigms of their hegemonic position in IR.

Shattering dominant state-centric understanding in IR, constructivism brought in ontological, ideational from reflexivity; methodological, epistemological understanding from rationalism. State-centric theories contend that human nature is destructive and thus causes war. Their understanding is often associated with the Hobbesian view of man as flawed and tainted by original sin.

The constructivist approach is often summed up by Alexander Wendt's assertion that *"anarchy is what states make of it"* (Wendt, 1992; 391). In this sense, Wendt is arguing that people act towards objects, including other actors, on the basis of meanings that objects have for them. For Wendt, IR is socially constructed and imbued with social values, assumptions and norms (Fierke, 2007). This appears to suggest that a state or NSA's understanding of anarchy will lead them to behave in particular ways in the social context of IR (Dornan, 2011).

Both theoretical approaches accept that the structure of IR is anarchical. However, there is a debate as to whether or not the effects of anarchy such as self-help can be overcome without fundamentally changing the structure of IR. Realists, such as Waltz argue that anarchy and its resulting security dilemma cannot be overcome unless a world government is created. On the other hand, constructivist dispute this approach arguing that anarchy itself does not explain the behaviour of the states but one needs to recognise the importance of identity, interests and inter-subjective understanding of these factors when seeking to explain IR (ibid).

Shattering the frangibility dominant state-centric understanding in IR, feminism revolutionised the study of IR, they said that IR is dominated by men. Concepts like sovereignty, security etc. are masculine dominated. The mainstream state-centric IR paradigm is epistemologically questioned by feminists where they say that the whole epistemological process in positivist is gendered.

Feminist scholars have attacked the assumptions of state-centric theories because it is purely based on the experience of males. Some feminist IR scholars like Jean Bethke, Cynthia Enloe and Tickner have argued that the core assumptions of state-centric theories, especially of anarchy and sovereignty, reflect the way in which males tend to interact and see the world. State-centric approach simply assumes male participants when discussing foreign policy decision making, state sovereignty and the use of military force. Tickner (2014) argues that Morgenthau's principles are embedded in the masculine perspective and

Morgenthau's Six Principles of Realism[10] is evidence of such masculine knowledge construction in IR.

Tickner's work on IR is based on the acknowledgement of the centrality of gender/human oppression. In her view, the discipline of IR was a decade old and still is largely synonymous with the state. This state is not based strictly in the personalities of individual male, but in hegemonic masculinity.[11]

Cynthia Enloe in her book *Bananas, Beaches and Bases* (1989), returns to a feminist standpoint interpretation to argue that women have always been inside IR through the practice of its politics such as diplomat's wives, assemblers of commodities, tourist bringing foreign exchange, consolers of soldiers based far from home etc.

---

10   Morgenthau's six principles of political realism: 1: Politics is governed by objective laws which have their root in human nature. 2: The key to understanding IR is the concept of interest defined in terms of power. 3: The forms and nature of state power will vary in time, place and context but the concept of interest remains consistent. 4: Universal moral principles do not guide state behavior, though state behavior will certainly have moral and ethical implications. 5: There is no universal agreed set of moral principles. 6: Intellectually, the political sphere is autonomous from every other sphere of human concern, whether they be legal, moral or economic.

11   Feminist Perspective in International Relations. Retrieved, December 2017. At https://sol.du.ac.in/mod/book/view. php?id=1345&chapterid=1088

Enloe states the problem as learning how the conduct of IR has depended on men's control of women.[12]

Feminists argue that all researchers are gendered and the way the researcher looks at it is from a gender perspective and this therefore makes research gendered. This also makes scientific community gendered which has a penetrated influence. This cannot isolate what the researcher does because it is paramount to the justification of a theory. If the scientific community is gendered then the paradigm they shape in IR is also gendered. For feminists, the whole objective reality is gendered which keeps people oppressed. Human beings are essentially gendered beings and this is what feminists are trying to break.

IR as a distinct subject is currently undergoing a phase of uncertainty. These uncertainties prove that there are major blind spots with respect to social and political change. This conceptual blindness frequently leads to empirical blindness. The recent events like 9/11 attacks have shocked the entire world community. Hence, it clearly requires a rethinking of the basic assumption of IR vocabulary which is dominated by state-centric theories.

It is comprehensible that the state-centric theories could not incorporate the role of other significant players in IR where theories like Critical Theory, feminism, constructivism etc. brought in a very new dynamic in

---

12   ibid.

the comprehension of IR. With the end of WWII and the emergence of the Cold War, IR was subjugated by the highly militarised and polarised ideological confrontation between the two superpowers. The rivalry and confrontation were intense, political and military concerns dominated the understanding in IR.

However, with the end of the Cold War, globalisation became a widespread phenomenon and international system witnessed momentous changes. The end of the Cold War witnessed a paradigm shift leading to a cobweb paradigm in IR. The understanding in IR was entangled with various assumptions and theories where each were trying to provide an analysis on the shift that was taking place in IR. The end of the Cold War also witnessed a power shift in two distinctive ways. The first is in a geographical sense, with power moving from certain traditional strong states such as U.K, the U.S to other states like China, Japan. The second is parallel where power is shifting from State to Non-State Actors (NSA). Parallel shift is more transformative and is considerably a different kind of shift. This movement or shift needs further theoretical consideration and analysis. In such circumstances, new actors have increased their involvement in IR. IR theories have traditionally been state-centric and territorially biased, with military power the ultimate arbiter. Non-State Actors (NSA) and Armed Non-State Actors by contrast, see the world comprised of overlapping networks, with influence their key weapon due to their relatively minimal military capabilities.

Conventional IR theories have paid scant attention to these outlier threats (Aydinli, 2016). As Daniel Drezner (2012), in conclusion to his unconventional examination of NSAs threats in IR noted,

> *"This sobering assessment highlights a flaw in the standard of International Relations Paradigm – their eroding analytical leverage over the security problems of the twenty-first century"* (Pierskalla and Hollenbach, 2013; 207).

The new war arguments revolve around changes in the means, methods, financing and actors of contemporary conflict. The actors are held to be NSAs frequently organised around a unifying identity. These armed groups use irregular strategies and tactics, including attacking civilians, assassination, bombings, and avoiding direct confrontation with the state army. This new war position in opposition to state-centric, ideologically motivated conflicts that mobilise the population (Thomson, 2014). The decline of inter-state war has changed the international system where the concept of war is undergoing a paradigm shift from old to a new war. Just-War Theory is no longer equipped to understand this new shift in the understanding of war where third generation warfare, irregular warfare[13] etc. have engulfed the understanding giving wider connotations to the

---

13 Irregular Warfare is defined as a violent struggle among state and non-state actors for legitimacy and influence over the relevant populations.

understanding of war. Similarly, there is a decline of the state where geographical and geostrategic factors have taken centre stage in understanding IR. This was actualised with the end of the Cold War and expansion of Neo-Liberalism in the form of globalisation in theorising world politics.

There is less comprehensive understanding of NSAs. If one agrees on a parallel shift then such transformation needs further theoretical analysis. Theories like constructivism, functionalism, neo-functionalism, liberalism etc. does incorporate NSAs role, but the importance of NSAs remains heavily entangled in various assumptions and analysis. These problems need to be addressed from an IR perspective.

Realism has frequently confronted states that have grown out of armed groups and revolutions, whether Mao's China, Bolsheviks in Russia, Fascists in Italy or National Socialists in Germany. Constructivist and Copenhagen School articulate the role of ideas and societal discourse in the process of securitisation, while noting the plethora of new security actors. Liberals have long examined the influence of NSAs in world politics, whether individuals or MNCs. It may be in Hedley Bull's understanding where it could give some amount of comprehension about NSAs. Hedley Bull discusses new medievalism as a situation characterised by a system of overlapping authority and multiple loyalty. This overlapping authority may take the form of the regional, world, or even sub-state or sub-national authority. Bull lists five features of contemporary world politics which provide evidence of such trend towards neo-medievalism, but states that whether or not it deprives the concept of sovereignty of its utility and viability is the key piece of evidence that the alternative neo-medieval system is actually occurring (Thomson, 2014).

Various analysis of the wave of globalisation on IR stresses the brewing importance and influence of NSAs in world politics. Frequently emphasised implication is the eroding ability of the state to fulfil the traditional purposes, such as national security and economic stability and prosperity. The apparent rise of NSAs as significant players in global politics has many consequences and it demands further theoretical analysis. The understanding that NSAs can have an affluent impact in IR, it connects to long-standing debates in IR theory and about how such players relate to the dynamic and structure of global politics. Paradigms that build NSAs into their comprehension does not incorporate what is happening with the rise of NSAs, particularly the increasing capability of these actors to exercise material capabilities vis-a-vis states and one another and the resulting impact of this ability on how ideas play a role in IR (Fidler, 2008).

Anarchy is one of the most significant concepts in IR theory. State-centric theories comprehend anarchy by focusing much on interactions of states, and they dismiss NSAs as factors in the state-centric analysis. Liberalism and constructivism does incorporate NSAs into their study and explains how NSAs influence anarchical politics. However, broader understanding has not been laid down to comprehend NSAs (ibid). One needs to understand the role of NSAs from a theoretical perspective that comprehends or analyse a broader understanding of NSAs, such paradigm lack in the study of IR.

As such state-centric understanding looked at IR from a single dimension and it has been insufficient to address changes taking place post the Cold War period. The mechanism used by states to address such changes has been inadequate because the challenges have grown far beyond the range of any state-centric analysis. In short, NSAs have become essential instruments within the international system. Today, it is difficult to analyse IR and behaviours of nation-states from the state-centric paradigm. As mentioned by Brown (1995), *"the world policy is the process of self-transformation out of the traditional nation-state system and into a system more congruent with the contemporary global polyarchy"* (Ataman, 2003; 59). The escalation of NSAs in world politics questions the state-centric paradigm in IR that doesn't comprehend wider implications of the escalation of NSA.

1.4 Theory of Open Source Anarchy (OSA)

To bring some much-needed clarity to understand global transformation and bring non-state entities into the study, Theory of Open Source Anarchy has been used to further understand NSAs role and its materialisation into ANSAs in world politics. Theory of OSA posits that anarchy, which was a closed concept in IR where only states participated, has now become open making room for NSA/ANSAs penetration.

The theory of OSA endeavours to explicate how and why anarchy today reflects the ability of many NSAs to develop and use material power in ways that affect IR. OSA states that anarchy is undergoing a transformation that presents states and NSAs with unprecedented governance challenges for which traditional approaches prove inadequate. Therefore, the understanding of the 21st century IR has to be looked from the prism of OSA.

For scholars of IR, anarchy describes a context where the political system recognises no common superior authority. Anarchy is the opposite of hierarchy – a political context in which the actors centralise power and create superior and inferior sources of authority. Conceptually speaking, politics within a state is hierarchical, but politics among states are anarchical.[14]

IR theories are acquainted with the idea that IR transpires in the condition of anarchy. However, the

---

14 The real world is mosaic than analytical concepts because we sometimes see more anarchy in domestic politics, such as occurs in failed states, than witnessed in the relation between sovereign States, such as the member states of the European Union.

theories in IR leave us with a different understanding of anarchy. All the prominent theories in IR posit that the behaviour of states or actors in the system is affected by anarchy. The state-centric outlook of realism etc. theorise anarchy as an exogenous, structural determinative of state behaviour. It is anarchy that drives the behaviour of states and responds to other states. For constructivism and liberalism, which comprehends the participation and impact of NSAs, anarchy reproduces the predilection and design of actors in IR. State-centric theories analyse state behaviour to understand the structure of IR, constructivism etc. starts with the behaviour of NSAs to understand how and why state performance in anarchy looks and functions as it does. The anarchical structure of international politics does not, therefore, necessarily determine patterns of behaviour for actors in the system. This approach allows analysis to take account of factors related to NSAs participation that state-centric discounts as irrelevant (Fidler, 2008).

The concept of Open Source Anarchy (OSA) was mounted by David P. Fidler where he borrows theoretical foundation from liberalism and constructivism to incorporate NSAs into the study of IR. The theory of OSA hypothesises that anarchy, as the essential characteristic of IR, has become accessible to NSAs as never before.[15]

---

15 The theory of Open-Source Anarchy also relates to the phenomena of small, weak States, such as failed States, having more impact on IR than in past historical periods.

This straight access has consequences and characteristic for world politics that the leading theories in IR do not explain well. State-centric paradigms in IR emphasises rational state calculations concerning their power and material capabilities, cannot explain destabilising, the violent threat posed by armed groups, terrorist groups or globally organised crime syndicates to state interests and stability without forcing these threats into traditional patterns of state-centric rivalries. Similarly, State-centric understanding struggles to understand and explain why powerful states like the U.S have to concern themselves with weak, failing states that become platforms for malevolent NSAs to threaten the interest of the powerful states (ibid).

State-centric paradigms have disregarded NSAs significance and created an illusion understanding that anarchy is accessible only to states. This means that anarchy is not natural but deliberately created to off-limit NSAs influence to states. Anarchy was looked from the lenses of the states and it can be found partly in the development of International Law where the fading of natural law made states as sole subjects and author of international law. International law became whatever the states wanted. The state-centric understanding of anarchy extended beyond international law and included the Balance of Power (BOP) where the dynamics encouraged the involvement of militarily, politically and economically powerful states reducing the involvement of NSAs in the dynamics. What states feared were not NSAs but ideological and religious forces. Even the economic activities of NSAs were looked from state-centric lenses. As suggested by the policy of Mercantilism, states calculated economic development and trade as elements of national power, translating what NSAs generated in their domestic and transnational economic activities into resources relevant to the competition states endured in IR (e.g. East India Company) (ibid).

The understanding of anarchy was mounted by states for their own interest, irrespective of their domestic government, cultural mores, ideological predilections and religious traditions – none of which substantially alters how anarchy functions. At a deeper level, state-centric paradigms cast doubts on whether states can alter anarchy much, even if they wished to do so, missing some catastrophic experience that splinters temporarily, the BOP (e.g. Rise of Napoleonic France, French Revolution etc.).

NSAs play a prominent role in IR and this argument attains theoretical background and OSA provides such background. It is clear that anarchy in IR was made a closed one accessible only to the states. The emergence of OSA entails control over anarchy. Anarchy is no longer the domain of the states. This change entails that material capabilities and ideas of NSAs provide states with undeviating access to sway how anarchy manoeuvres.

The state-centric approach to anarchy bears a resemblance to an oligopolistic market in which small number of superior powers determine demand and supply of power and ideas in anarchy. Superior power dominates in oligopolistic anarchy because they have achieved economies of scale in the production and use of material capabilities, particularly military power, that render them relatively invulnerable to competition from weaker states to NSAs (ibid).

The relationship between ideas and power in anarchy is inelastic. Alterations in ideas have no influence on the pattern of power among states or how states configure their methodology to their interests or power. The great powers have such compensation in terms of material capabilities that weaker states and NSAs face redoubtable barriers to influencing the dynamics and structure of anarchy. Idea formation and normative activism do not cease, but it has little to no impact on the machinations of great powers in oligopolistic anarchy. Now, to revolutionise oligopolistic anarchy and permit NSAs to influence anarchy requires considerably changing or altering the material conditions of competitions among actors. Moving from an inelastic to a more elastic relationship between power and ideas in anarchy requires; greatly reduced competition among states for power and transformations that allow NSA to develop greater material capabilities in IR (ibid).

The apparent escalation of NSAs in IR overlaps with; the rise of U.S as a hegemonic power after the demise of USSR and technological enlargement that have permitted NSAs to enhance their material capabilities for engaging in IR. The dramatic change in the structure of competition for material power among states, combined with the diffusion of material capabilities to NSAs through technological transformations, opened the condition of anarchy to more direct and independent access by various NSAs. Through this access, NSAs have more impact on how anarchy functions (ibid).

The expansion of OSA is consequently a purpose or a function of technological and structural changes that considerably lessened the barriers to access for NSAs and independently and directly affect the state of anarchy that epitomises IR. These changes also developed the relationship between ideas and power more elastic. Changes in material capacities of NSAs and states actors have a further substantial effect on the world of ideas in OSA than state-centric outlook. Normative and ideational ferment typically trails noteworthy structural changes in the equilibrium of material power in IR. The explosion of normative activity has been taking place since the historic period from Napoleonic wars that produced Holy Alliance, Congress of Vienna similarly the end of WWI produced League of Nations (LON) and then again United Nations (UN) after WWII.

Such events produced a normative activity but more importantly it was during post the Cold War period that normative activities took off consistently. Liberal trading regimes expanded in the form of WTO, responsibility to protect was expanded, democracy-liberalism-globalisation became widespread, human security emerged as a new concept, expansion of public private property, civil society, International Criminal Court etc. explicates how normative activity expanded. The disintegration of USSR left U.S foreign policy in need of new concepts, tactics and strategies (ibid). Ironically, quasi-hegemonic supremacy structure greatly amplified the elasticity between ideas and power in IR and NSAs opportunity to influence global politics.

A revealing instance of such new elasticity appears from the therapy or treatment of HIV/AIDS pandemic after the Cold War. The disease continued to enlarge and the U.S government became increasingly concerned about this problem and started to think about it. The disease was manifesting itself with the U.S policy and it reflected new elasticity between power and ideas triggered by the collapse of the bipolar Balance of Power (BOP) system. This elasticity continued to appear in further developments on HIV/AIDS, including discussion of this problem before the Security Council, the targeting of HIV in the Millennium Development Goals and establishment of global fund to fight AIDS, Tuberculosis and Malaria, and the controversies on developing country access to patented antiretroviral treatments in the context of the WTO's agreement on IPR (ibid). No better example of the growth and use of material power by NSAs can be found on ANSAs. ANSAs repeated attack across the globe, alliances, online recruitments etc. have dramatically affected foreign policy of other countries. ANSAs had accessed anarchy and influenced its dynamics in ways that many states could never imagine accomplishing. ISIS also illustrates the elasticity of power and ideas in OSA.

OSA posits an elastic relationship between power and ideas in which NSA/ANSAs directly participate, thus affecting in various ways on how anarchy operates. This type of anarchy reflects changes in the distribution of material power among NSA/ANSAs and states that creates more space for NSA/ANSAs to participate directly and indirectly in IR. The increased prominence of NSAs in post-Cold War period flows from the combination of the end of the rigid, bipolar BOP system of the Cold War and technological and other transformations that allowed NSA to develop greater material capabilities for participating in global politics (ibid). OSA is a recent phenomenon made possible by the combination of structural transformations effected by the end of the Cold War and contemporaneous convergence of technological transformations that increased NSA/ANSA material capabilities to engage in world affairs (ibid).

1.5 Non-State Actors (NSA) in IR

It is apparent that Non-State Actors (NSA) have attracted various narratives in IR as it is clear that the state-centric theories do not incorporate NSAs. Open Source Anarchy (OSA) has exclusively incorporated NSAs into their study and their role in world politics.

The equilibrium between states and NSAs has shifted over the past 30–40 years (Josselin and Wallace, 2001). When globalisation became a widespread phenomenon, NSA's access over investment, communication, trade etc. expanded while the cost of doing these things have also reduced. Over the past three decades, the explosion of NGO, MNC, banks, and economic associations has also increased.

State and NSAs are opposing forces but analysing NSAs without analysing state would be misleading. Far from reinforcing the conventional argument of the realists, that the NSA is subordinate to states, this might suggest that one looks at the history of the modern international system. In the first instance, this would suggest looking at the history of the state itself. First, the state as we know it today, as the powerful entity controlling the territory, economy and population it rules, is a recent creation, a product of modernity of the nineteenth and twentieth centuries. If this is so, then the residual, or supposedly recent, 'non-state' is in fact a continuation of something that prevailed until this modern state was formed. In today's pre-modern society, much of that is controlled by the state which was administered by other entities – the family, the religious group, the tribe, the local lord.[16]

---

16 It is a matter of ethical and sociological debate how far such pre-modern institutions, many transnational constituted a civil society: independent of States they were, Democratic they were not.

The corrosion of the Westphalian system rest upon contemporary illusion as the question of NSAs to the Westphalian system itself is a mistaken concept. If one looks at the history of such nationalism, ideologies, religion or socialism, one can see how far the NSA has been present. WWI, WWII, the Cold War etc. had fundamental NSAs dynamics in it: Bolshevik insurgents in Petrograd, Serbian assassins at Sarajevo, Fascist in Munich and Rome, the massive swathe of nationalist from the third world and insurgencies of communist 1940s to 1980s, civil and national protest movement that emasculated European communism. The whole history can therefore be written from a non-state perspective (ibid).

The assessment of the past may therefore allow to pose a spirit of enquiry. The question of how far the history of the system, far from being one of the states or of the kings and queens who ruled them, is in fact a history of non-state (ibid). First, reformation of theology and forerunners of wars in the seventieth century that led to the treatise of Westphalia: here ideas, religious movements, individuals and also the interest of state played their part. Second, it was not the states who explored but historians, philosophers etc. who were non-state entities. During the Cold War and end of the Cold War, states were major players, so were NSAs, such as social and religious movements, peasant movement, anti-communist movements, working class etc. played a major role. The understanding of history is widely based on states but NSAs also played their part in evolving history i.e. Scientific Revolution, Industrial Revolution, Renaissance period and French Revolution (ibid).

NSA is a very diverse universe. Theoretical inclusion of Karl Marx and Liberals has NSA aspect in it. In IR, it is clear that the definition dates back to the theoretical debate of the discourse. Academic research of Mitrani (1994), Ernest Has (1964), Karl Deutsch (1990) on the pluralistic notion of transnational linkages has shown the way. Work on complex multilateralism is closely associated with transnationalism (Aydinli, 2016). It is apparent that NSAs took centre stage on the facet of globalisation and expanded post the Cold War period. The idea of transnationalism has come back with a new study on the wave of NSA with the theory of OSA.

Over the past few decades, NSA has increasingly affected the social change i.e. climate change, human rights etc. NSA as a mediator in conflict resolution as seen during the US-Iran nuclear deal which was mediated by International Atomic Energy Agency (IAEA). World Trade Organisation (WTO) and the World Bank have become a mediator in the international dispute. Business groups such as Information Technology (IT), Multi-National Corporation (MNC), Communication have expanded. Press and Media also play a role in influencing the foreign policy of countries.

Direct links to domestic policy of states, national policy making, language and access to international institutions have become NSA sources of influence. NSA also follow the tactic of cultural homogenisation, democratisations etc. The emerging concept of civil society has also shaped the idea where diasporas issue such as formation of Liberation Tigers of Tamil Eelam (LTTE), radical separatist groups like Uzbek rebels etc. further developed the understanding of NSA (Wallace and Josselin, 2001). But the question on how independent these transnational actors are still needs an answer and it needs further conceptualisation from an IR perspective.

The increasing number of international organisations is parallel to increasing level of economic, political, social and cultural transactions between individuals, societies and states. The growth of many kinds of NSA challenges the state-centric concept of IR and replaces with a transnational system in which relationships are more complex. The proliferation of NSAs has recently led some observers of IR to conclude that states are declining in importance and NSAs are gaining more importance. New theories such as OSA by Fidler (2008), complex interdependence by Keohane and Nye (1997) were formed to explain new developments. International Institutions habitually organises global conferences on the status of the environment, the status of women, human security, businesses etc. So, NSA has learnt to penetrate space between multilateral institutions and member states, developing a triangular relationship of complex multilateralism where social groups and economic associations are also substantial players (ibid).

NSAs are principally autonomous from state structure and machinery and also autonomous from Governmental and inter-governmental bodies above and below the formally sovereign states transnational rather than trans-governmental. Some actors are transnational where they operate on a cross-border basis, pursue some set of goals everywhere and address a global audience. According to Wallace and Josselin (2001), NSAs include organisations that are essentially autonomous from government control, funding and beyond state control. It operates in the network which is cross-border and engages in transnational relations linking society, political system and economy. It acts in a way affecting political scenario either one or more states or international institutions. It is comprehensible that NSAs is a wide universe that needs further investigation. In such entangled analysis Muhittin Atamanin his article "*The impact of Non-State Actors on World Politics: A challenge to nation-states*" (2003) classifies types of NSAs in global politics.

Following the classification of NSAs, Ataman points out that there are two types of NSAs; first, NSAs that are created by states, second, NSAs that are established by certain social groups, individuals, businessmen and others (Ataman, 2003).

1.5.1 International Inter-Governmental Organisations (IGOs)

International Inter-Governmental Organisations (IGOs) are deliberate associations of sovereign states instituted to fulfil various objectives where states look forward to cooperation through a sort of prescribed structure and to which states are not capable of realising by themselves. The number of IGOs has substantially increased in their particular fields. They are fashioned by agreements which mirror inclination of stronger states. Stronger states create IGOs because they require them to protect their foothold. Consequently, they are an element of Westphalian state system where IGOs are instruments of nation-states. IGOs can be categorised by function (environmental, social, political and economic) and by scope (regional and global). IGOs are accessory of nation-states and play substantial roles by bestowing means of communication and cooperation. It is sympathised that the main purpose or functions of IGOs are agenda setting, rulemaking and information gathering (Brown, 1995).

IGOs track standards, rules of international institutions and regimes in states i.e. IAEA monitors non-proliferation of atomic weapons. The UN plays a prominent role in countries obtaining information about international politics and society. Functionaries of IGOs like the IMF and UN are crucial for countries UN Security Council and IMF are significant organisations where some influential states monitor activities of organisations and necessitate their standards selectively (ibid). For example, the UN Security Council cannot acknowledge any verdict against permanent members and their allies.[17]

1.5.2 International Non-Governmental Organisations (INGOs)

NGOs are organisations that are set up by NSAs. There are numerous NGOs such as government organised, the government initiated, transnational, industry and business, operational, transnational social movements, anti-governmental NGOs etc. They have become a decisive contributor in international policy processes, they participate in IGOs discussions by organising new issues, supporting IGO development, building transnational social coalitions, improving skills in diplomacy etc. They promote inter-state cooperation by educating delegates, preparing background papers and reports, serves as third-party source of information, facilitating agreements etc.

NGOs which operate at transnational level have become more significant determinants of the foreign policy of countries. Like their counterparts that operates at domestic level and lobby in their respective countries, they lobby at international and transnational levels. Human rights advocates, gender activists, religious movements, developmentalists and indigenous people

---

17   Security Council decision on Palestinian inquiry against Israel has been vetoed by the U.S.

have invaded the territory of nation-states (ibid). As pointed out by *Brown*(1995),

> *"as the countries and sectors of world society have become more and more interdependent, it has become commonplace for non-governmental groups representing similar communities in their various countries to closely coordinate their policies and to constitute themselves as INGOs"* (ibid; *276*).

1.5.3 Multi-national Corporations (MNCs)

The most significant contemporaneous NGOs are MNCs. They are colossal firms that control and own offices in more than one country and sell their merchandise and services across the globe. They are massive corporations having subsidiaries and branches operating worldwide simultaneously.

MNCs are major drivers of global economic integration and establish unprecedented linkages among economies worldwide. The biggest and the most effective industrial corporations are based in the U.S, Europe and Japan. In 1992, of the twenty largest MNCs, excluding trading companies, in terms of sales all were based in G-7 states – eight were in the U.S, four were in Japan, three were in Germany, and five were in Britain, two of which were jointly based in the Netherlands (Goldstein, 1999). MNC can be categorised respectively to their kinds of activities they are into such as, agriculture, transportation, extractive resources, industrial products, tourism and banking. The most distinguished are financial and industrial corporations where their primary purpose is the maximisation of profits (Ataman, 2003).

MNCs are very competent in directing the foreign policy of nations, including that of the most powerful ones, and they set agenda for international politics. They have become a major factor in national economic decision making. They have enormous flexibility in moving money, personnel, goods and technology beyond national boundaries and this flexibility increases their bargaining power with governments. For example, MNCs like Exxon, General Motors, Royal Dutch Shell, General Electric and Hitachi outranked the GDP of countries like Taiwan, Norway, Pakistan, Turkey, Argentina and Nigeria. As compared to total world export in 1992 of about $4.0 trillion (ibid), sales by MNCs outside their countries of origin were $5.5 trillion (ibid) for the same year (ibid).

MNCs serve the interest of countries where they belong to as a mechanism of economic development and a device of diplomacy. They are extremely centralised and subjugated by a parent company which is located in the home country. The supervisors are from home country, technology is imported from the home country, research is centralised, profits are often repatriated and the policies of the firm conform closely to the economic and foreign policies of the home government. Therefore, Wallenstein's Dependency

Theory (1970) and A.G Frank's World System Theory(1984) considered MNCs as instruments of neo-colonialism. MNCs increase production in the home country to supply components for foreign subsidiaries. They can ensure lower-priced products from the foreign subsidies back to home (ibid). They heavily influence financial, economic, political and social policies of home and country abroad. In short, they determine foreign policy and domestic policies too. However, there are many conflicts between MNCs and their home countries over taxation, trade policies and economic sanctions. MNCs may not want to follow national policies pursued by their home governments (ibid).

1.5.4 Humanitarian and Religious Organisations

Human rights are traditionally understood to regulate certain relations between individuals and nation-states. This understanding has changed significantly after WWII. Even though state-centric and sovereignty based conception of the World System remains the norm for international human rights, nation-states are now obliged to obey transnational and international formal and informal legal and political constraints on their human rights practices. Nation-States have to take into consideration international and transnational public opinion since there are dozens of transnational organisations that monitor human rights practices of nation-states and examples of coercive foreign intervention (ibid).

A distinguished instance of the international human rights regime is represented by the Council of Europe. The Economic Commission of Human Rights receives, reviews and evaluates complaints from individuals living in the member states and the European Court of Human Rights makes legally binding decisions (ibid).

Amnesty International (AI), International Red Cross and International Red Crescent are prominent and significant NGOs in human rights monitoring organisation worldwide. International Red Cross and International Red Crescent assist during wartime and sends aid to man-made and natural disasters. They work along with UN bodies. AI on the other hand tracks areas where human rights violations are taking place. It commences campaigns against states violating human rights (ibid). European Parliament uses AI's report to formulate its policies like the European Parliament's policies towards former Yugoslavian states regarding human rights violations and issues. Green Peace for instance, is another significant actor of the environment. It protests against the policies of countries that affect the environment. It has prevented many policies of states concerning the environment. It has also assisted in sponsoring environmental programmes in small countries (ibid).

Political and Economic scholars mention that there were substantial religious groups and movements that had a significant impact on IR. Roman Catholic Church is one of them. It was a major force in the middle ages superior to Kings and Emperors. Although it lost its supremacy with renaissance, enlightenment period and others, its significance as a transnational actor continued. The institutional structure of the Catholic Church, the most enduring of transnational actors, reflect both on competitiveness from nation-states, and norms and expectations that are derived from the Church itself. It has been supporting democratic opposition movements initiated by Catholic Christians such as in Poland, Latin American Countries, Sudan, Northern Ireland, Indonesia and others. Many statements and visits made by the Pope strongly influence international politics (ibid).

1.6 Intricacy in Defining NSA

There is an intricacy in defining NSA and the bewilderment prevails in understanding defining and categorising NSA. State and NSAs are divergent but when there is state analysis NSAs automatically fits in or the other way round. State provides support to NSAs like banks, NGOs, MNCs etc. to perceive help from such NSA in many forms. It could be policy influencing, fund collection, business contracts, trade etc. On the other hand there are groups which are seen as a threat by the state. The state is consistently threatened by armed groups such as Hezbollah, Boko Harem, Al-Qaeda etc. There are NSAs that are fully autonomous such as armed groups operating in transnational and others. Also there are NSAs that are semi-autonomous and operates with the assist of nation-states. Such NSAs includes NGOs, MNC, Armed Groups etc. Now the confusion is state participation in the operation of NSAs that are deemed autonomous. There is autonomous NSA that emerged out of state activities such as ISIS, Al-Qaeda etc. but they are now understood as autonomous NSA without state control. Such a mystification is something that has not been addressed properly.

NSAs that fall under the framework of state-centric are NGOs, MNCs etc. as they are dependent on the state. They lobby, pay taxes and are a part of International Treatise. They have an affiliation to the state. Illicit NSA in this regard is the most autonomous NSA and they have their own interest. The organised groups as long as their financial interest is secured, remain loyal to the state. Politically driven groups however look to overthrow state system at a broader level. This act has led to harsh treatment.

As we have already discussed before how power is shifting from state to NSA or Static to Non-Static. So, when the state feels that a certain NSA are of their benefit then a transfer of power may take place which is known as *persuasion*. If a state trusts an NSA and gives them certain power then it is understood as *trust*. If a state is unable to provide services and NSA emerges as an alternative and challenges state, it is known as *apathy*.

It is now apparent that power is transferring from state to NSA. Apathy is something that needs to be understood from an IR perspective (Aydinli, 2016)

It is lucid that there is an intricacy in defining NSA so a new approach or an outlook has to be followed to understand the wider role played by NSA. Clear concepts have not yet been tracked in defining NSA. The understanding attracts complexity. The understanding of NSA attracts intricacy where various scholars have opposing views in defining NSA. Huntington defined Clash of Civilisations (1997) as NSA (Josselin and Wallace, 2001). Biersteker's (1987) understanding was based on types of authority and William Wallace and Josselin (2001) defined NSA based on transnationalism (Aydinli, 2016). There are various framework laid down in understanding NSA. Some looks at the capacity of implementing policy and decision, shared interest, values, principles, shared norms, goals, autonomy etc. this understanding gives a framework for the analysis of NSAs. However, the problem still lies in defining violent groups, terror threats, organised crime etc. Similarly, there is also a struggle to explain why influential countries like U.S, U.K, France, Britain, Russia etc. have to concern themselves with the weak, failing states that become breeding ground for Armed NSAs threatening their existence itself. The framework in which NSA has been laid doesn't explain these emerging threats. Therefore it has to be looked from a different perspective.

1.7 Armed Non-State Actors (ANSAs)

After the end of the Cold War, threat perception has shifted from states to NSAs and within NSAs it further shifted towards violent NSAs from statist to non-statist. Researchers have often been biased in understanding NSAs so they tend to overlook threat posed by violent NSAs. This happens when they are theorised with liberal understanding. A possible reason for avoiding research on violent NSA is because the researcher considers it as a part of terrorism studies, studies on organised crime etc. so there are very few works on violent NSA because of marginalisation. Intelligibility in understanding NSA has transpired into further understanding of NSA using violent means. As the early elucidation makes it clear on how intricacy prevails in understanding NSA using violent means because of entangled analysis on NSA where both state and NSA goes parallel. It has become obligatory that the shift in threat perception to NSA and further materialisation into armed NSA have to be scrutinised. Power transition which takes places at three levels: Persuasion, trust and apathy have shown how power is shifting from static to non-static, such conversion comprehends 21st Century threat posed by NSA using violent means which is often understood as Armed Non-State Actors or violent Non-State Actors (ibid).

Rather than focusing more on power transition, the threat-centric strand includes work focusing more on non-state threats itself such as terrorism, transnational violent activities of NSA and organised crime have to be looked upon. Sub-section of what we might consider as threat-centric inquiries on ANSA comes out of terrorism studies, and particularly the inquiry into new terrorism. Even though the new terrorism debate is far from achieving consensus, one critical distinction that has made new and old terrorism is the ability of new terrorist groups that survive globally in the international system despite persistent persecution by the state or by states (Pillar, 2001) therefore distinguishing contemporary transnational capacity which is substantially different in nature as it neither requires nor receives state sponsorship.

In a broader understanding of NSAs, a number of works featured in the era of 9/11 or post 9/11. Distinguished appeared those by Oliver Roy (2002), Rohan Gunaratna (2002) and those comprehended from the perspective of counter-terrorism such as Steve Coll (2008), Michael Scheurer (2004) etc. further conceptualised NSAs in much broader ways by focusing more on their transnational, they have explained new phenomena materialising out of NSAs and Terrorism Studies within the Islamic Tradition. Works of these scholars comprehend an understanding of ANSA and of Ersel Aydinli (2016) in particular focuses more on ANSA and its transnational activities. David P. Fidler (2008) has shown direction on how NSAs threat has changed the outlook moving away from state analysis. Similarly Peter G. Thomson (2014) precisely indicates armed group threats that have provided further analysis on ANSA in world politics. However, it was after 9/11 attacks more work started to appear on violent NSA but limited. Terms Armed Non-State Actors and Violent Non-State Actors can be used interchangeably. When an NSA uses a violent means, it is understood as ANSA or VNSA. It is an augmentation of independent transnational activities of Non-State Armed Groups. ANSA is an organisation that uses violence[18] to fulfil its goals. In various countries, ANSA not only intimidates business, corrupt politicians and launder their proceeds, but also engage in a range of activities that defy and weaken state sovereignty. In most of the African countries as well as Asia and all across the globe, ANSA is a major player in the political system.

There is no universally agreed definition on ANSA. However, the term is used to indicate organised armed entities that are primarily motivated by political goals, operating outside effective state control and lack legal capacity to become a party to international treaties. ANSA are coherent, autonomous NSA that relies on use of force to achieve their objectives. This definition does not spell out types, degree of independence and internal and external dynamic of ANSA. In order to comprehend role played by ANSA one has to look into their types, degree of independence and internal and external dynamics.

---

18   Violence as force not approved of by the recognized State/States

1.7.1 *De-Facto* Governing Authorities

De-Facto governing authorities are understood as a body that have attained partial autonomy but not recognised as a separate entity that can become a member of international bodies like UN and International Treatise. Kurdistan, which is often called as de-facto[19] region is located in West Asia where the region is officially governed by its own autonomous groups like People's Protection Unit (YPG), Democratic Union Party (PYD) etc. who is now fighting against ISIS in the region. Kurds have asked for a separate state of Kurdistan which is not yet recognised by countries across the region and the globe. They got the de-facto recognition after 1991 when Iraqi forces left the region. Such de-facto governing authorities are often linked with ANSA because of their transnational activities and they are not a recognised state entity that uses force so it is associated with ANSA.

1.7.2 National Liberation Movements (NLMs)

People identify themselves and give loyalty to ethno-national groups apart from nation-state. Many individuals pledge their allegiances to ethno-national group that shares a common language, civilisation and

---

19 Recognition de facto implies that there is some doubt as the long term viability of the Government is in question. It involves a hesitant assessment of the situation, an attitude of wait and see to be succeeded by De Jure recognition.

cultural tradition not to the government and state that controls them. As a result of their allegiance to ethnic groups, NLM are rapidly gaining momentum in global politics. Most of the countries are multi-ethnic and includes minority issues too, such rising momentum of ethnic groups reduces the magnitude of nation-states in IR.

NLM is playing a significant role in IR for decades, especially in Asia, Latin America and Africa. One of the most acknowledged NLM that still plays a prominent role is Palestinian Liberation Organisation (PLO) and has been playing a key role in Arab-Israeli conflict. Arab states had, for a long time regarded Yasser Arafat as a representative of the Palestinian population across the globe. African National Congress (ANC) under Nelson Mandela was another significant NLM that disintegrated white superior authority in the country. Patriotic Front of Rhodesia and Southwest African People's Organisation (SWAPO) of Namibia illustrates significance of NLM in world politics as these NLMs shaped or demarcated African Continent and also their political structure (Brown, 1995).

Stateless nations, nation without states or nation or ethnic groups without a state are also very significant actors in international politics. Even though there are 3000 to 5000 nations in the world, if a nation is defined as a population with a distinctive and enduring collective identity based on cultural traits and ways of life that matter to them and others to whom they interact, there are only less than 200 nation-states (ibid). Some nations without state that are vigorous players or actors in IR are the Catholics in Northern Island, Palestinians in West Asia, the Catalonians and Basques in Spain, Tibetans and Muslims in China, the Quebecois in Canada, Muslims of Serbia and Kurds in West Asia.

1.7.3 Transnational Criminal Organisations (TCOs)

TCO are transnational in both their operations and organisational structure, engaging in illegal activities frequently using illegal means, which use corruption and violence to further their objectives and protect their operation. Most TCO maintains autonomy and clandestine in nature in keeping with general armed group characteristics. The more publicly TCO generates, whether through spectacularly violent operations, large scale or relatively high-visibility illicit activities such as human trafficking, drug trafficking etc. the more likely state will face pressure from lawmakers, the domestic population and international observers to crack down on the illicit behaviours and groups that perpetuate them (Thomson, 2014). There is no single structure under which TCO operate and that these groups may change and evolve between there organisational structure (ibid).

Traditionally, TCO were viewed as hierarchical organisation with mob bosses and the heads of mafia families, resembling a firm's CEO. The consequences of having a clear leadership structure were assumed to be that law enforcement could remove the leadership and the group would fall apart. But in many cases, TCOs have proven much more resilient for three main reasons. First, hierarchical TCOs had clear line of succession. Second, TCOs proved adaptable and flexible in the face of increased government pressure, engaging in new illicit activities and transferring assets and wealth to new markets and regions. Third, any one TCO is less important than market. After Colombian forces killed Medellin cartel leader Pablo Escobar in 1993, other cartels were able to supply cocaine market. TCOs are outward manifestation of deeper political social and economic problems. TCOs use violence in order to protect their turf and markets and to intimidate and deter both rivals and government. They also uses violence to maintain internal discipline and prevent defection. The level of violence varies based on expected government and rival actions, as well as TCOs objectives and organisational structure. TCOs may constrain excessive violence, which invites greater government scrutiny. Furthermore, levels of violence may not accurately indicate criminal activity, as the better organised the crime, the less violence associated with it (ibid).

TCO have been engaged in number of illegal economic activities which are predatory, market based and commercial crimes. Predatory crime are those based on theft, such as identify theft and maritime piracy.

Market based crimes are those based on counterfeiting and trafficking, including currency counterfeiting and trafficking in narcotics, small arms, people and cigarette. Lastly, commercial crimes are those based on tax evasion, regulatory violations and criminal negligence. TCOs and other armed groups may also commonly engage in crimes including kidnapping, bribery, and subversion to further their goals of increasing their profits (ibid).

Los Zetas, a Mexican TCO, was originally composed of deserters from Mexico's Special Airmobile Group (GAFE), who acted as a Gulf cartels private paramilitary force. They carried out assassinations, arms trafficking, human trafficking, and protected drug trafficking routes, eventually moving on to controlling large swaths of territory on behalf of the Gulf cartel. The group split from the Gulf cartel sometime between 2008–2010 after hiring themselves out to other cartels.[20] Today, they are one of the largest and most violent cartels in Mexico and maintain cocaine-trafficking networks through Central America. They have hired former Guatemalan special forces soldiers (Los Kaibiles) as part of their effort to maintain a highly trained membership while increasing their control over Guatemalan trafficking. Los Zetas operate in Mexico, Guatemala and US, as well as traffic drugs through several West African states bound

---

20 Congressional Research Service.2013. *Mexico's Drug Trafficking Organisation: Source and Scope of the Violence* Reittel. Congressional Research Service.pp 15.

for Europe. In 2009, President Obama added Los Zetas to the list of traffickers and organisations subject to violence against Homeland Security.[21]

1.7.4 Non-State Armed Groups

Non-State Armed Groups consist of small population or membership with lack of legitimacy and sovereignty; they are clandestine in nature and operate in transnational level. These include groups that are armed and fight against the state repressive policy for their survival and accomplish their demands or requirements. These includes groups like Boko Harem, Al-Qaeda, Uyghur Liberation Organisation (ULO), Jeemah Islamiyah (JI) etc. who operates without state influence and fight against state's repression policy.

1.8 Autonomy, Representation and Influence (ARI) Framework

Armed Non-State Actors can be looked at from ARI framework. It is lucid that ANSA includes Anarchist, TCOs, NLMs, de-facto governing authorities etc. It therefore includes all armed groups in comprehending

---

21 The White House, Office of Press Secretary, "Fact Sheet: Overview of the Foreign Narcotics Kingpin Designation," June 10, 2017, http://www.whitehouse.gov/the_press_office/ Fact-Sheet-Overview-of-the-Foreign-Nacrotics-Kingpin-Designation-Act.

typologies which is in a way very contested. Consequently there is a problem in further conceptualising ANSA and understand its non-statehood. Therefore ARI framework has to be looked upon here to disentangle such bewilderment. In order to analyse ANSA and their role in global politics/IR, one has to look at ARI framework. ARI provides a common point for discussing, comparing and analysing the global actors of different ANSA. ANSA may have minimal autonomy but high influence or high autonomy and low influence, ANSA who are autonomous maintains good balance of representation and displays compelling and transformative capacity that constitutes influence and has potential to affect IR.

1.8.1 Autonomy

Autonomy is more to do with distinction of ANSA in particular from state/states. State can be categorised as Failed, Quasi-state etc. Similarly, ANSA is not a concept but it can be seen as moving along with a spectrum from relatively more statist to more non-statist. Variation of actors along these spectrum can be looked at from two perspective. A: Distance from the state B: Distance from state-centric regime (Aydinli, 2016).

Distance from the state: More the distant from the state, more free will be ANSA. This does not mean that ANSA is very strong. In fact, ANSA may use state as a support system for financial aid, infrastructure, arms aid, state's territory as a base for fighting e.g.: Houthi Rebels in Yemen being funded by Iran. They may be beholden to any case. In such cases, ANSA could be said to have very low autonomy. Similarly, if an ethnic violent group receives financial or other support from targeted state they will have less autonomy.

ANSA who is able to find their own alternative financial background then it is considered to be more autonomous than the previous one. Another is being able to survive state's repression policy and being able to survive without state's support. In this, second one is considered distinguish aspect of ANSA. Another is active and passive ANSA. Active are those that can defend themselves and passive are the ones who exist free from state's influence. Most ANSA have been in a mixed state in this regard as one can take an example of Al-Qaeda where it gained much support during Afghan War and was very limited after 9/11 (ibid). But such groups also are able to disperse and go underground as seen after 9/11 and also regroup later e.g.: AQ expansion of its network (AQAP, AQIP, AQIM etc.).

Distant from state-centric regime: ANSA distant from state-centric regime can be considered from two interrelated perspectives. First, how well ANSA is able to create new and alternative regime instruments by transferring money using legal to fund illegal e.g.: Osama Bin Laden. Second, how well the ANSA is able to manipulate weaknesses of the state-centric regime in order to ease its own functioning. Groups like ISIS, AQ etc. are anti-state and then statist (ibid).

1.8.2 Representation

Having a common identity among members serves the essential purpose of creating a relatively unified actor then identify its priorities and policies. But it has the added role of serving the group's own regeneration potential which is necessary for its survival. ANSA must work to maintain its members and attract new ones (ibid). Therefore, the first measurement of representation is ANSAs ability to continuously supply constituents to keep it active and meaningful. ANSA does not require to represent capacity but also critical factors that may support or limit such recruitment; the scope of potential recruits and to generate loyalty among its members to keep them committed. Jihadist for instance is mixed when it comes to regeneration as being globally dispersed constituency, albeit religious/sectarian on the definition of potential members and audience.

Rather than focusing on recruitment strategies and tactics for recruitment, one has to look at underlying support mechanisms for recruitment capacity. First is the scope of potential recruits. ANSAs regeneration potential is automatically limited if the range of possible group members is narrowly defined. For instance, if an ANSA is in nature restricted to a particular ethnic group or geographical location then membership is limited. Another is if an ANSA is ideologically defined whether on the basis of religious or political ideology, the potential recruits become colossal. Second is the support mechanism for recognition and legitimacy.

ANSA must build up recognition and legitimacy among its members e.g.: meeting the requirement of member's security, financial reward, defending member's religion or ideology. For meeting such demands require illicit actions such as the use of resources appropriated illicitly from one market to fund illegal activities in another, such acts may allow them to improve their legitimacy. The jihadist armed groups use the latest technology effectively in recruitment and propaganda. Dissemination of message is mostly done through the internet, publications and personal communication.

Now, it should be pointed out that gaining recognition and legitimacy whether through violent or non-violent means has ramifications for both the representation and influence factor in this framework. In terms of influence, legitimacy increases when states feel obliged to respond to and thus recognised the ANSA.

Greater the loyalty, more the group will be able to maintain its representation and the greater its potential role may be in IR. There is always a shift from state to NSA/ANSA. So, when such a shift is taking place, is it possible of shifting loyalties in a shift polity power?

Traditional loyalties to state are always under threat, groups/people tend to shift their loyalties to the NSA. Ethnicity and religion are principal identification factor of differences, therefore ethnicity attracts dual supports. In ANSA, ideological factor produces sustainable loyalties. They use dogmatic and religiously inspired belief system which is for them is the right cause and victory.

With wide regeneration success, ANSA will become very large and diverse that it will become difficult to manage effectively. If it becomes diverse then it may be very difficult ideologically and physically to control, it can then be divided. ANSA with a more narrowly focused scope and objectives, aims etc. e.g.: ethnic-based ANSA are less likely to face a greater risk of outstretching. ANSA with global aims and scope like the jihadist will have the problem of outstretching management because of increasing operational independence via ideologically bounded local cells around the globe.

At the concrete organisational level, a high level of expansion means greater challenges. For ANSA, smart way of handling this is by keeping distant cells or fractions connected for communication and exchange which opens ANSA up to easier establishment and penetration. Outstretch may occur on a more ideological level. With rapid growth, it becomes difficult for ANSA to maintain operational cohesiveness. With more members and sub-groups, agreeing on a common code of conduct, target selection, strategies and even acts are most appropriate for achieving more goals.

A serious issue for ANSA is outstretching issues of actual ideological cohesiveness, since divergence on this front speaks to every identity of groups. e.g.: in early recruitment during the 1980's in Afghan. They were more willing to ignore basic so differences among the recruits grew and evolved around Islam. This led to the differences in fighters. Turkish jihadist disapproved religiosity of

Saudis and Yemenis. To cope up with this, Osama had to keep various jihadist groups separated physically while trying to keep them on the same ideological rope. The ideological cohesiveness is mixed for the jihadist armed groups. Very dogmatic ideology helps in management but practices and interpretation are still differ (ISIS and Boko Harem actions being condemned by AQ leadership).

1.8.3 Influence

All ANSA influences IR through agile stateless and resourceful networks. ANSA could have influence if it shows evidence of constituting transformative and compelling challenges to states and statist system. Sustainability is something that has to be looked upon. Two things come here; First; being based on deterrent free motivation. Second; having adequate flexibility and adaptability (ibid). For ANSA to be sustainable, its constituency must be motivated by a force that is deterrent free. The presence and future members of ANSA must be driven by an idea that will continue to motivate them in action even in the face of extreme resistance from states (ibid). Such strong motivation will stem from money, illicit authority, criminal activities, ideology etc. The sustainability for Islamic ANSA or the jihadist is very high because of their motivation being linked with religion and belief in the right cause.

In case of formidable opposition from the state, ANSA is more likely to survive if it makes rapid significant changes in everything from strategy to tactics to organisation. E.g.: Popular Front for the Liberation of Palestine (PELF) made an abrupt shift after 2001, when it chose to adopt a religious ideology. A move made partly because of the realisation that with a secularist ideology, it was failing to recruit suicide bombers, the most influential means of action.

The way by which ANSA can be flexible and adaptable is by wielding transnational space as a medium for basic functions crucial to sustainability. E.g. having sources of security, exchange and empowerment ANSA looks for location and space that are less accessible for states. The flexibility and adaptability of Islamic armed groups are high because of the constant evolution of recruitment, planning and organisational methods. They are also simultaneously transnational and localisation are very effectively operated or managed.

Transnational space includes physical spaces (failed states) and non-physical (cyberspace). ANSA may resort to these transnational spaces for security purposes, exchange ideas, know-how, resources etc. such exchanges may be done in physical transnational space or non-physical.

Empowerment is another area that might most effectively take place in transnational spaces. Transnational space has now become resourceful for empowerment and armament—E.G. Al-Qaeda network. Today there are 638 million (ibid) illegal arms circulation.

ANSA influence comes down to impact that it holds. A: the degree to which the ANSA impact is compelling. B: the degree to which it is transformative. First one is where the state is compelled to act against ANSA which is negative recognition. Positive recognition on other hand is where the state recognises NSA and its role. E.g. semi-autonomous NSA, de-facto region etc. Unrecognised ANSA uses violent means to be recognised by the state. For financially motivated ANSA, violent doesn't work. For politically motivated ANSA, violent works perfectly. E.g. suicide bombers recognised as violent NSA. Suicide terror increases their success rate. Weapons of Mass Destruction (WMD) have become their main focus as it was seen during Syrian Case as how they break down state-society relationship with such activity (ibid).

ANSAs with global transformative influence would be one that presents credible threatening capacity. States today struggle to confront ANSAs impact in IR. Traditional International Law and norms prescribed under UN Charter concern themselves only with the use of for by state against the sovereign, territorial integrity or independence of another state as drafted in Article 2 (4) of the UN Charter. If state behaviour changes with ANSAs act in IR then ANSAs can be said to be the most influential actor in IR. E.g.: AQ compelled the US to overrun the UN and NATO. Presence of another group ISIS leads to unlikely cooperation not only between states like Iran, US etc. but also state and non-state relations are being intensified such as the

US supporting Syrian Kurds, Russia supporting non-ISIS jihadist and finally a change in the relation between US, Turkey, Saudi Arabia etc.

1.9 Conclusion

The understanding of IR had been biased with the state-centric approach and its theories such as realism. It was in 1970s new approached emerged in IR that looked at other actors operating apart from the state being considered a major player in IR. Theories like Critical Theory, constructivism etc. brought in a new dimension in understanding IR. In 1991 with the end of the Cold War NSA emerged as a significant player in IR which the leading theories does not incorporate NSA as a new player in the global arena. The analysis of NSA was a confused one entangled with various theories and assumption. In such mystification, the theory of OSA brought in NSA role in the global arena by addressing how NSAs are shaping IR by entering anarchy by using material power and capabilities. Theory of OSA has helped to look beyond the state-centric approach towards NSA.

The understanding of NSA attracts intricacy because of the state's involvement in influencing NSA policies and role in IR. Although MNCs, TNCs, humanitarian groups etc. comes under the prism of NSA influencing global politics, their transnational role has been questioned and NSA itself not being able to throw explication on armed groups that alter state/states policies and IR. NSAs have further materialised into ANSA that have gained glared of publicity only after 9/11. Studies relating to ANSA hit the centre stage after 9/11. TCOs, NLMs, Anarchists etc. are considered as ANSA although their categorisation has not yet been verbalised. The independence of ANSAs has been questioned and therefore it has to be looked from an ARI framework which provides an analysis of how independent are ANSA from the state-centric approach. By looking at the ARI framework it is lucid that jihadist armed groups like AQ, Boko Harem etc. are the most independent ANSA.

Chapter II

ISIS as an Armed Non-State Actor

2.1 Introduction

Dealing usefully with ideological /revolutionary ANSAs, it requires us to disentangle how a particular ANSA is inclined with one ideology. Over several decades, we have seen that Islam has spread in a transnational manner where various ANSAs are epitomised by Islam and its interpretation that followed over several years. Transnational links of Islam have roots in its succeeding party that took over after the death of Prophet Mohammed. Division within Islam and its spreading process across the globe have created a different ideological belief within Islam. Various scholars and activists did take part in spreading different belief system in Islam. The Islamic fundamentalist interpretation of various thinkers and activists like Muhammad Ibn al – Wahhab, Ayatollah Khoemini, Osama Bin Laden et al. have given ANSA an Islamic ideological base to carry out their operation. ANSAs like Boko Harem, Al-Qaeda (AQ), Hezbollah etc. have borrowed interpretation from these activists and thinkers and carries out their operation with such Islamic base. ISISs ideological awakening lies in the radical interpretation of Syed Abdul A'la Mawdudi, Jamal Ad-din al-Afghani, Syed Qutb et al. ISIS organisational foundation and evolution has a long history that traces back from Soviet intervention of Afghanistan to Arab Awakening.

This chapter makes an attempt to understand Islam and its transnational links and Islamic ideological base of ANSA and how ISIS came into being and evolved to be known as the most formidable ANSA.

2.2 Islam and Its Transnational Links

Islam has been associated with politics from the very inception of its history. Prophet Muhammad set up a political authority rather than simply preaching a religious message (Dalacourain Wallace and Josselin, 2001). Similarly Christianity has also been a part of European politics all through its history but Islam has remained as a political tool and heavily politicised religion in the modern era where there is an extensive political secularisation. The term 'political Islam' or 'Islamism' or 'Islamic fundamentalism' fits to describe such phenomenon and differentiate Islam as an ideology, providing a set of social and political guidelines, from Islam as a religion, practised by millions of people in an apolitical fashion.

Islam was employed by established kingdoms like the Ummayyad Dynasty, Abbasid Dynasty, Sasanian Empires etc. to legitimise and strengthen their rule since its inception. Now it is frequently used for the opposite purposes, taken up by opponents of Dictators in West Asian countries to challenge and overthrow established governments. This ambivalence of Islam in relation to authority and government continues in the modern period. Islamism[22] poses a serious challenge to political authority. Islamism, and especially Islamic fundamentalism, based on the notion that the *umma* must overcome the state because it is an artificial creation which fragments natural unity of believers, questions the very foundation of the political establishment in West Asia. It also facilitates the creation of transnational links between Islamist movements that link up societies and bypass governments. The challenge to the state is therefore both ideological and political (Dalacoura in Wallace and Josselin, 2001).

Transnational links are an old phenomenon in Islam: networks between orthodox *ulama* (religious leaders) and *Sufis* (mystical sects) have always crisscrossed political boundaries in West Asia and even beyond. But Islam as a modern political movement has a symbolic beginning in the figure of Islamic fundamentalist thinkers and scholars

---

22　An advocate or supporter of a political movement that favors reordering government and society in accordance with law prescribed in Islam.

that have traversed the West Asia region preaching their fundamentalist approach in the form of Islamist movements.[23]

Most of such movements in West Asia revised the legacy of radical Islamic fundamentalism while others remained adherents to a political Islam of a moderate and flexible nature. However, it is irrefutable that Islamist movements in West Asia have spread very quickly in a transnational manner, through a network of intellectual and political contacts between societies (George in Sidahmen and Ehteshami, 1996). The initial phase of the extension of political Islam was from the 1930s to the 1950s. The Muslim Brotherhood of Egypt which was established by Hassan al Banna in 1928 rose to political prominence in the 1930s and 1940s. The brothers also volunteered in the first war against Israel in 1948. The *mufti* of Jerusalem was the leader of the Palestinian cause and crucial link between it and Muslims beyond (Dalacoura in Wallace and Josselin, 2001). The obscure of political Islam coincides with Nasser and Arab nationalism from the 1950s. However, the contemporary emergence of political Islam in West Asia took place in 1967 defeat by Israel, this symbolised the damage of reputation of Arab states and their Arab nation. The failure to fight and reoccupy Arab homeland created frustration among

---

23 Islamic Fundamentalism and ideological root of Jihadist will be covered in next topic.

the Arab Nations and Islamist movements. In such predicament Islamist movements used Islam as a political tool for their cause. With the Iranian Revolution of 1979, Islamism arrived at the peak in West Asia (ibid).

Islamism sees the modern state as illegitimate because, according to their ideology, sovereignty must rest with God, not the people. They also believe that the *umma* must come together over and against the state. Fundamentalists like Sayid Qutb and Syed Abdul A'la Mawdudi were the major ideologues of the contemporary Islamist movements. They wrote and spoke on the corruption of contemporary governments in West Asia and the decline of the Muslim world. Their solution was restitution of Islamic governments and the re-imposition of *Sharia*. The circulation of ideas through numerous publications, messages, videos, meetings, conferences etc. has been crucial in spreading Islamist message to the movements across West Asia. Most connections between Islamists movements across state boundaries are of crucial, social and political nature. These movements have engaged in a series of transnational causes to which they have contributed funds and volunteers, the first being Palestine. The invasion of Afghanistan by the USSR in 1979 and the establishment of a communist regime made Afghanistan a major centre. Bosnia and the fate of Muslims in former Yugoslavia was a major concern.

Chechnya in the late 1990s has also been the cause. There are vital connections between these causes. International networks exist which have continued to recruit one jihad after another (Roy, 1998). After the termination of war against USSR, training camps for *mujaheddin* was never closed down. The Taliban movement which controlled Afghanistan at the end of the millennium has boasted of the existence of these camps which train Islamists from across West Asia. Islamic networks operating out of this war-torn country have become interlinked with smuggling mafias (Dalacoura in Wallace and Josselin, 2001).

There is a state link in some of these movements or groups as Saudi Arabia also less publicly supported variety of groups throughout the Muslim world. It is impossible to track the extent of these financial subventions and to whom they are directed, and the degree of Saudi involvement is certainly overstated. Yet, there is no doubt that Saudis have, at various times, provided assistance to groups such as *Ikwan al-Muslimun* in Egypt and Jordan, *Jama'at-I Islami* in South Asia and Britain, *Hizb-I Islami* in Afghanistan, *Jama'at Nasr al-Islam* in Nigeria, and the *Warith ad-Din*-led Islamism in the US (Eickelman and Piscatori, 1996). Islamic Militancy in West Asia stems to a large extent from *madrasas* that have appeared in great numbers in certain countries like Afghanistan, Pakistan and Saudi is a huge contributor to such schools (Roy, 1998). From this account it is lucid that some amount of state intervention or support mechanism has featured in such ANSA.[24]

There is also some evidence to suggest that a network of Islamist charities and relief groups may be part of the vital supply lines of radical activities targeted against the West. Western countries, notably the US were the objects of armed attacks. Former USSR is also the target of Islamic armed jihadist through their vast lands especially operating from Central Asian countries and Caucasus (Dalacoura in Wallace and Josselin, 2001). China's *Xinjiang* province has also been engulfed with such activities where series of attacks have taken place operated by the armed separatist *Uyghurs*. Much has been made of transnational networks in ANSAs epitomised by Islamic interpretation such as Al-Qaeda, ISIS, Boko Harem etc. for cross-border influences through communication, recruitment etc. these range of cross-border flows of activities and ANSA themselves as seen in countries like Yemen, Saudi Arabia, Syria, Iraq, Lebanon and Islamic Maghreb have made significant impact in IR.

In order to recognise wider applicability of such ANSAs in IR and understand its wider role, one has to

---

24 The autonomy of ANSA has been discussed in the previous chapter using *ARI* framework. In this particular situation of funding by the States, such ANSA are considered as less autonomous compared to the ones who does not depend on State for financial support. They are not fully autonomous but some amount of autonomy does exist in such groups.

look into Islamic fundamentalism and various scholars associated with it. One needs to comprehend wider connotation of ideological base looking at various scholars and how the concept of Islamic fundamentalism evolved over a period of time that gave an ideological base in a transnational manner for the Islamic movements and ANSA in particular.

2.3 Islamic Ideological Base of ANSAs

Islamic ideology has provided a definition of the problem that ANSA faces. This can be ethnic or religious persecution, loss of sacred homeland, marginalisation etc. ANSA leaders who have adopted radical Islamic interpretation are frequently able to motivate ANSA based on their identity. This is done by relying on the Islamic ideological framework that is used to undergrid the group (Thomson, 2014). When an ANSA is fuelled with radical Islamic interpretation, then their activities will also get associated with such radical interpretation.

While contemplating conflicts in the contemporary world from the 9/11 attacks to the current Syrian crisis, it is lucid that ANSAs driven by radical Islamic interpretation have emerged as significant players in IR. Various interpretations of Islamic values and ideals have produced several approaches to IR such as political theology, sectarian, ethnic, national and cultural. Thus, there is multiplicity in Islamic ideology.

Although the complexity in understanding Islamic ideological base remains, Sunnah, Siyar and Qur'an have remained as an ultimate law giver to Islamic societies and the notion of Ummah has continued to shape political thought in Islam. All Islamic societies have these things in common. The sovereign states, NSA/ANSAs operate revolving around the principle of community feelings. It is often observed that these actors compete for hegemonic positions. For instance, countries like Syria, Iraq, Iran etc. fighting against ISIS. Another example of actors competing for the hegemonic position would be ISIS war against Al-Qaeda over territory possession in Iraq and Syria. Current situation of Yemen where there is a tug of war between Houthi rebels and Yemeni government also highlights actors competing for the hegemonic position.

The actors competing for a hegemonic position in the Arab World may share some theological background but their belief system is contradictory. For Sunni, the world is divided between the house of Islam and the house of war/enemy, these two are in perpetual conflict. For Shia, the world is based on Qur'anic message and the world for them is divided between the house of the oppressor and the oppressed. These various contest on the prospect of defining boundaries of Ummah serves more confusion in developing a single ideological base for ANSA.

As Turner in his article *"Islam as a theory of IR"* (2012), points out three key principles from where developing an understanding on Islamic ideological base is possible. First, the state and sovereignty as embodied by Ummah are linked by asabiyyah (solidarity). Second, the inside/outside the domain of Dar-al-Islam and Dar al-Harb and in between domain of Dar al-sulh or Dar al-Ahd (covenant or agreement). Third, the ontological belief in God (Allah), the revealed message Qur'an, and the traditions (Sunna) of Prophet based on his saying and practices. These principles are applicable to approaches of traditional, non-traditional and the salafi/jihadist but it differs on certain usage of their applicability (Turner, 2012; 13).

Contemplating Turner's (2012) understanding of Islamic IR, it is possible to develop an understanding of Islamic ideological base of ANSAs and how it evolved over a period of time. Three distinctive ideology of Islam (traditional, non-traditional and jihadi/salafi) emerges when one examines Islamic thought. To understand the Islamic ideological base of ANSAs, the three concepts (traditional, non-traditional and jihadi/salafi) becomes defining components of Islamic ideology.

2.3.1 The Traditional Approach

Jihad defines traditional school. For them, the world is divided into Dar al-Harb (the realm of war) and Dar-al-Islam (the realm of Islam). Here, a very distinct concept of foreign relations as defined by the constant struggle for survival is evident. The Dar al-Islam is those areas under Islamic control where the rights of Muslims are observed and ruled by a true Muslim. The world beyond this domain is Dar al-Harb. This domain is not just considered dangerous and threatening as a classical realist theorist may conceptualise anarchy, but it is considered a space which can be justifiably conquered in the name of spreading the religion under the appropriate conditions (Kazleh, 2006). For a substantial time span, the concept of Dar al-Islam and Dar al-Harb defined foreign relations in the Islamic world.

Traditional philosophy comprises strict epistemological establishment based on textual and literalist inquiry. The Qur'an and Hadith are the initial points of investigation in this school of Islamic ideology. The traditional school believes that Qur'an is the word of God which was spoken to the Prophet Muhammad by Gabriel angel. Hadith for them are the deeds and words of Prophet himself. Hadith and Qur'an are the pure formations of knowledge and therefore they are not subjected to amendments. For them, Islam is the absolute political, economic and social which is divinely given. Traditionalist interprets that Qur'an and the Hadith are the ultimate guides to understand the ontological aspect of civilisations.

In Islamic ideology, the concept of sovereignty does not exist, they believe in Ummah which for them is a unity of community that binds the Islamic world together. It is invisibly bound by assabiya.

Although, the traditional approach has been criticised for being static in their concept of foreign affairs, they remain however very influential in modern Islamic thought (ibid). The philosophy of traditionalists has remained influential among the revivalist who believes that western concepts have been imposed upon them and their world surrendering Islamic belief system. This makes the traditional concept of jihad as equipment for survival in a world full of aggressive forces where there is a struggle for power that has threatened the existence of Ummah.

Hasan al Banna's Muslim Brotherhood (MB) founded in 1928 is an ideal example of ANSA following traditional interpretation of Islam. Sayyid Qutb, who was an influential personality of Muslim Brotherhood exhibits traditionalist realist attitude by calling for the restoration of Sharia law through physical power and jihad. In his work, *In the Shade of Qur'an* written during 1951–1965, Qutb confronts some of the most profound problems of contemporary life for which he proposes an Islamic solution. The centred problem of modern society, he maintains, is a spiritual improvement that has caused deep unhappiness even among those who have most benefitted from scientific progress and economic prosperity. The answer for Qutb is a revolutionary Islamic transformation based on the rule of God and divine law as codified in Sharia. Such restructuring of society would free people from human masters, human laws and false values (Perry and Marvin, 2008).

Muslim Brotherhood abides by the interpretation of the traditional approach. They believe that Islamic governments must strictly be based on Qur'an and Hadith to create a perfect political and social organisation. For the Muslim Brotherhood, the notion of sovereignty revolves around the concept of Ummah which is a physical territory and can only be unified with Islamic law and caliphate. Muslim Brotherhood is an embodiment of traditional interpretation of Islam.

2.3.2 Non-Traditional Approach

The non-traditional approach was the outcome of the late 19th and 20th Century debate. When Traditionalists were confined to Islamic revivalism and Islamism, non-traditional approach emerged. Non-Traditional approach is influenced by Jamal ad-din al-Afghani who rose to a mediated position between the Zealot wing of rejectionist position and modernists incorporating western ideas (Turner, 2012). Afghani's works are considered as emblematic of an endeavour to find a middle path between Islam under customary clerics, and the West, as promoted through imperial projects. His fundamental thesis was that Islam's embrace of modernity should not imply a wholesale acceptance of secular principles or norms (Edwards, 2013).

Non-Traditional approach believes that Islam has been de-islamised with the wave of modernity. In response to such transformation escalating in the Islamic world, they argue for the third way, the concept that of Dar al-Ahd (the realm of treaties) for the possibility of peace with the non-Muslim world.

The non-traditional approach differs from the traditional approach in terms of epistemology and methodology. They do not subscribe to inside-out domains because they believe it was constructed during the conquest period when ideas of Hellenic world penetrated the Islamic society. Although, both traditional and non-traditional believe in Qur'an and Hadith, they differ when it comes to ijtihad. Non-traditional regards ijtihad as a legitimate source of method of knowledge particularly in dealing with matters that are not covered in Qur'an and Hadith. They make this argument with an understanding that modernity is necessary but the Islamic world should not follow it with absolutism and they should not mirror the west (Turner, 2012).

ANSAs like Hezbollah and Hamas represents non-traditional thoughts. They are influenced by Afghani, Abduh and Ayatollah Khoemini's work whose approach is the nucleus to wasatiya (middle way). Their work reflected on a reform that would restore Islamic civilisations with some modernity involved in it, but not at the cost of Islam. They argued for the creation of new jurisprudence that could welcome change as well as preserve traditional belief and culture. For them, cooperation between the Muslims and Non-Muslims was necessary if the order is to be maintained and achieved (Barker, 2005) Hezbollah followed the concept of Dar al-Adh after the group entered Lebanese politics after securing eleven of the thirty cabinet positions, with veto power (Nortion, 2007). Similarly Hamas is also involved with peace-making in West Bank and Gaza strip where the group signed treaties with Fatah.[25] This demonstrates that Hamas and Hezbollah, although they possess arms and ammunition for survival, they are an embodiment of non-traditional interpretation.

2.3.3 Salafi/Jihadi Approach

Just like the traditional IR theories emerged out of various debates and challenges with changing nature of global politics. In a similar manner Islamic ideology has evolved with changing nature of IR. As we have seen earlier, the traditional approach was a product of Islam's formidable years characterised by persistent conflict, first defensive and later offensive. As Islam struggled to survive, a particular attitude was entrenched in the minds of Islamic scholars (Turner, 2012). Islam was closely linked with survival and war. It was more like theoretical and hypothetical Hobbesian state where there was insecurity for external survival because of the nature of the struggle

---

25   April 2014 Gaza Agreement and September 2014 Hamas Fatah Agreement.

that defined human understanding and characteristics. In the same way, the emergence of non-traditional thinking was a product of European encounters and penetration of modernity. Now that the world has entered a new stage with the end of the Cold War, how must we look at such transformation from an Islamic perspective?

The contemporary understanding of Islamic interpretation can be understood as engaging in a debate that would speak for the Islamic world to define itself. The salafi/jihadi thinking developed out of global conflicts where the interests of the west and the Islamic world have coincided amounting to conflicts. One can simple argue this by looking at how western education, ideas, beliefs etc. have penetrated the Islamic world. People have been forced to accept regimes that are installed by western powers which were seen in countries like Iraq where Shia regime was installed after toppling Saddam Hussein, making Sunni minority in the country; salafi/Jihadi is a response to it. A salafi/jihadi school is more than ideology; it is an evolution within Islamic interpretation influenced by traditional and non-traditional.

Salafi/Jihadi schools seek to bring in a change in IR. The 9/11 attack is a symbol of such change where Al-Qaeda epitomised by the salafi/jihadi interpretation featured the headlines across the globe. The term Salafism is derived from an Arabic term salaf, meaning righteous predecessors. It is like Islamic revivalist concepts that speak of an idealised Islamic world (Turner, 2012).

The salafi/Jihadi interpretation seeks to rediscover original Islam through holy texts. They adhere to several tenents of classical such as rejection of modernity and nation-state system (Adiong, 2016). Ibn Taymiyyah, was the first one who contributed to this thinking. He was a major leader in the revivalist campaign to open doors of ijtihad (reformation). Ibn Taymiyyah distrusted human intellect as a reliable means of attaining religious truth, and rejected the arguments and ideas of both Sufis and other philosophers (Maqsood, 1994).

Muhammad Ibn al-Wahhab is another thinker who contributed to the salafi/jihadi interpretation. He started the Wahhabi movement where he drew upon the writings of Tamiyyah and came up with reformation and argued for a strict interpretation of Sunni Islam. He believed that Muslims who are engaged in other practices like Sufism, polytheism, mysticism, Shi'ism etc. were idolatrous practices. Moreover, he precipitated a series of confrontation by calling on his neighbours to change their practices and embrace his interpretation of Islam (Stern and Berger, 2015).

Abul A'la Mawdudi is regarded as one of the founding ideologues and figure of the salafi/jihadi interpretation. For him, Islam is a revolutionary ideology which seeks to alter the social order in the entire world and rebuild it in conformity with its own tenets and ideas. As he points out:

> *"There is no doubt that all the Prophets of Allah, without exception, were Revolutionary Leaders and the illustrious Prophet Muhammad was the greatest Revolutionary Leader of all"* (Ahmad, 1997; 8–9).

Abu Musab al-Suri, is subsequently associated with jihadi/salafi interpretation. His book *"Call to Global Islamic Resistance"* (nd) has frequently been linked to a manifesto and sporadically referred to as Mein Kampf of the Jihadi movement. Suri, in his book analyses the situation in IR where he argues that superiority, injustice, vulnerability, distrust and helplessness have marginalised Muslims across the globe. In response to such atrocities by the West, Suri argues that Muslims across the globe should unite for a Global Jihad (Masoud, 2013). Suri's interpretation of Global Islamic Resistance has acted as a template for jihadi movement across the globe where youths magnetised by his interpretation are joining jihadi groups.

ANSAs like Al-Qaeda, Boko Harem, Jemmah Islamyah etc. are the embodiment of the salafi/jihadi interpretation. These groups are influenced by the writings of Ibn Taymiyyah, Abu Musab al-Suri, Abul A'la Mawdudi, Muhammad Ibn al-Wahhab et al. ANSA group leaders such as Osama Bin Laden and others have also contributed to jihadi/salafi interpretation. Osama Bin Laden believed that national borders are western imperialist creations that serve to divide Muslims, he focuses on Ummah, as his revolutionary unit. For him, the physical symbol of Islamic civilisation is the caliphate that he aims to restore, perhaps with the expectation that he would become caliph. Restoration of the caliphate is only a prelude to the re-conquest of all lands that were once under Muslim rule. Ultimately, Bin Laden envisions a future where the entire world will live under Islamic law (Perry and Marvin, 2008).

After his constant attacks on the U.S. after 9/11, bombings of American embassies in Kenya and Tanzania (ibid), he said

> *"There is now no longer any debate about three well acknowledged and commonly agreed on facts that require no further proof, but we will repeat them so that the people remember them. Firstly, for over seven years America has occupied the holiest parts of the Islamic lands, the Arabian Peninsula, plundering its wealth, dictating to its leaders, humiliating its people, terrorising its neighbours and turning its bases there into a spearhead with which to fight the neighbouring Muslim peoples... There is no clearer proof than America's excessive aggression against the people of Iraq, using the Peninsula as a base. It is true that all its leaders have rejected such use of their lands, but they are powerless. Secondly, despite the great devastation inflicted upon Iraqi people at the hands of Judeo-Crusader alliance, and despite the terrible number of deaths over one million—despite all this, the Americans are trying to repeat these horrific massacres again... Thirdly, while these wars are being*

> *waged by the Americans for religious and economic purposes, they also serve the interests of a petty Jewish state, diverting attention from its occupation of Jerusalem and its murder of Muslims there"* (Perry and Marvin, 2008; 45).

Such jihadi/salafi interpretation of Ibn Taymiyyah, Abu Musab al-Suri, Abul A'la Mawdudi, Muhammad Ibn al-Wahhab, Osama Bin Laden et al. have radicalised other ANSA with such interpretation that has become Islamic ideological base of ANSAs like Boko Harem, Jemmah Islamyah, ISIS etc. Post 9/11 period has witnessed an evolution within jihadi/salafi interpretation, such evolution is carried out by ISIS. ISIS has brought a new interpretation to radicalise youths from the entire countries. They have applied ijtihad for waging war against the west. In order to understand ISIS interpretation and evolutionary characteristic within the salafi/jihadi school and ANSA, one has to understand the emergence of ISIS as an ANSA.

2.4 Rise of ISIS as an ANSA

In the 21st century, ANSA has emerged in large parts because of the growing weaknesses of many states that they seek to perpetuate and intensify. The notion of weak states, of course is inherently relative. When strong-weak continuum of states becomes exploitative then the panorama for the escalation of ANSA are substantially cultivated. For ANSAs like ISIS, they have succeeded in penetrating the weakness of the state's key dimension such as legitimacy, capacity, collective interest etc. Perhaps the best way to understand the rise of ISIS, therefore, is in terms of political fragmentation in West Asia that opened doors for jihadi/salafi interpretation.

ISIS life dates back in 1999 as a training camp in Afghanistan where Abu Musab Al-Zarqawi was a leading figure for the jihadist group Tawid w'al Jihad. However, Zarqawi's radicalisation into Islamic fundamentalist interpretation began in prison after being convicted of drug possession and sexual assaults. It is not hard to understand why Zarqawi would become infected with Islamic fundamentalist interpretation in prison (Hosken, 2015). He was a troubled man living in Jordan. In September 1970, King Hussein of Jordan waged war with Palestinian Liberal Organisation (PLO), a conflict that led to the expulsion of thousands of refugees and PLO fighters. In the following decades, political Islam featured in the shape of the transnational organisation the Muslim Brotherhood became significantly dominant in Jordan, taking over universities and other important institutions. Thus the Jordanian political context in the 1980s was like a nutritious broth in which Islamic organisations and radical currents proliferated (Bisard, 2005).

Zarqawi also attended for religious instructions in Mosques, principally the al-Husayn Ben Ali mosque in the Jordanian capital, Amman (Hosken, 2015) where his belief on Islamic practices and fundamentalist interpretation was accelerated. He then took the fateful decision to travel to Afghanistan, where he came in contact with the Mujahidin, and AQ and its charismatic leader, *Osama Bin Laden* (ibid). He did inherit Bin Laden's interpretation of Islam,[26] but it was his meeting with Abu Muhammad al-Maqdisi that made a significant ramification.

Born in 1959, Abu Muhammad al-Maqdisi became one of the most influential Islamist scholars in West Asia. To many jihadists, Maqdisi has been as extremely important spiritual leader and ideologue. Eighteen publications by Maqdisi were found among the effects of Mohammed Atta, the leader of 9/11 attacks (Brisard, 2005). Maqdisi is responsible for the ruthless and intolerant ideology followed by ISIS. Maqdisi's influence helped Zarqawi to become a radical; Jean Charles Brisard has described him like thousand times more dangerous than Zarqawi (ibid). Maqdisi introduced an impressionable twenty-three-year-old Zarqawi to an extremely puritanical form of Islam. Zarqawi and Maqdisi became unlikely friends, the star ideologue and intellectual and the one-time hoodlum and drunk. Together they proved to be a lethal concoction of ideology and extreme brutality. According to another Zarqawi biographer, Loretta Napoleoni, the ideology mixed with anger running through Zarqawi's veins horribly simplified the

---

26 See *Bin Laden's* Islamic Interpretation that has been discussed under Islamic Ideological base of ANSA.

word for him: *takfir* (the act of declaring someone as an unbeliever) was his response to consumerism and rapid modernisation that had destroyed the Bedouin way of life (Hosken, 2015). Zarqawi and Maqdisi served four years of their sentence together before being released in 1999, it was during this epoch that Zarqawi moulded further his terrifying character, recruited followers and prepared for a life of jihad (ibid).

In 1999, Zarqawi returned to Pakistan and by the end of the year he crossed the border and entered Afghanistan where the country was in control of the Taliban. In the southern city of Kandahar at the Government Guest House, he met Bin Laden. At first Bin Laden was highly suspicious of Zarqawi because of his hatred towards the Shia community and other sects. Zarqawi wanted to build a jihadi army he could lead anywhere but he needed support from AQ. Ultimately he was given 5000 pounds by AQ and allowed to set up his desert training camp near Herat, Afghanistan's third biggest city. It was called Tawid w'al Jihad, the Organisation of Monotheism and Jihad. Tawid's initial mission statement was to overthrow of the government of Jordan as well as the annihilation of Jews all over the world.[27] However, with increasing attacks of AQ and attacks of September 11, Bin Laden knew that U.S would strike back as U.S engagement in West Asia and NATO expansion was seen during this period where

---

27 See In particular. *Jordan Times*, 27 July 2003, based on the testimony in court of Shadi Mohammad Mustafa Abdullah.

Turkey was made a base for NATO involvement in the region. This made AQ restless and believed that operation could not be carried out with U.S involvement in the region. With this, Bin Laden focused on Iraqi Kurdistan which was an autonomous region out of reach of Saddam Hussein's regime, then still President of Iraq.

A small group of salafi militants had already established themselves in Kurdistan long before Bin Laden saw this area as a possible safe haven for jihadist in the wake of 9/11 (Hosken, 2015). On 1st September 2001, under the auspices of Bin Laden and Zarqawi, two Kurdish jihadi groups merged to form a new jihadi group named Jund al-Islam and were soon renamed as Ansar al-Islam. Soon the group began receiving Zarqawi fighters from Afghanistan to carry out a more effective operation in the de-facto region of Iraq, Kurdistan. It was later claimed that Bin Laden gave the group $300,000 (Bisard, 2005).

In mid-September 2001, around fifty-seven Arab-Afghan mujahedeen belonging to Zarqawi entered Iraqi Kurdistan via Iran. Although Zarqawi initially remained in Afghanistan making his fighters travel to Kurdistan, later when Afghanistan was under attack by U.S led coalition, Zarqawi fled to Iraq to start his new operation. As Zarqawi's fighters having already joined the group in Iraqi Kurdistan made him easier to control the group with his command. In no time Ansar al-Islam declared war on the ruling Patriotic Unit of Kurdistan to have complete control of the region (Hosken, 2015). Zarqawi also established another training camp in the province of Halabja. He established a laboratory for the manufacture of biological weapons. Later the U.S would claim Zarqawi's camp and presence in Iraqi Kurdistan as evidence of Saddam Hussein's complicity in the manufacturing of WMD (ibid).

To understand the rise of Zarqawi and later its materialisation into ISIS, it is crucial to understand Saddam Hussein's policy. Under Saddam Hussein, the Ba'ath Party had progressively hollowed out and ingested all-important state, political and civil society institutions (Sissions and al-Saiedi, 2013), and membership in the party was required for power, advancement and privileges. Initially, membership of the party was low until Saddam Hussein followed the policy of Ba'athification. His policy of Ba'athification was very progressive towards accelerating members of his party. He did this by paying them in huge amounts once they join the party. Ba'athists could be paid up to fifty times the pitiful wage rates prevalent in the public sector. A non-Ba'athist primary teacher would be paid around $3 a month whereas Ba'athist in the same post would be $150 (Allawi, 2007). Saddam's policy clearly opened up party membership which grew in short period of time. By the time of the invasion of 2003, membership was estimated at around 6,00,000 (Ricks, 2006), of which an estimated 15,000–40,000 were considered to be senior members (ibid).

Many people had joined the party out of fear and pressurised, it was also not possible to get a job without being a member of the Ba'ath Party. The most dangerous problem was that minorities especially the Sunnis had joined the party because of marginalisation. Most of these people were in high posts especially military and security services. As the invasion followed in 2003, American diplomat L. Paul Bremer III was asked to promote the development of a functioning democracy that could be returned to Iraq soon (Hosken, 2015). Being a top diplomat and representative of American interest in Iraqi soil, Bremer came up with the policy of De-Ba'athification. The De-Ba'thification degree declared that senior party members were removed from their positions and banned from future employment in the public sector (ibid). Bremer's policy simply excavated deep into public and private life of Iraqi people and further triggered tension between the Sunni minority and Shia majority.

Bremer's second degree was also to have far-reaching consequences that are still being felt today. On 23rd May 2003, Provisional Order Number 2 proclaimed that *dissolution of entities* that included the army and all armed services, associated militias, three government ministries involved with security, including the ministry of defence, as well as all intelligence bodies. It was a breath-taking dismantling of Iraq's security and intelligence infrastructure, and it involved the wholesale dismissal of thousands of military officers and security officials. Every soldier or security official was dismissed effective of 16th April 2003. In total, more than 7,00,000

(Ricks, 2006) people were fired, including 3,85,000 (ibid) Iraqi armed forces personnel and nearly 3,00,000 (ibid) interior security staff. Such mayhem created a political vacuum in Iraqi politics and functioning of the government. When Saddam was in power, he would not allow jihadi movements to thrive in Iraqi land. Soon after the invasion followed with the toppling of Saddam Hussein, Zarqawi was able to operate without any hindrance.

In 2003, Tawid w'al Jihad under the command of Zarqawi was on loose to freely operate in Iraq. They targeted Americans and their allies but above all they started a genocidal war against Shia. Apart from Zarqawi's group, there were other groups operating. Army of the Men of the Naqshbandi Order was one such group consisting of former Ba'ath members who were forced to leave with the policy called out by Bremer. 1920 Revolution Brigades was essentially a salafi group who played a crucial role after the toppling of Saddam Hussein (Hosken, 2015). They targeted mainly US troops with shootings, kidnapping and bombings, although they would later join the US in the war against ISIS. Jamat Ansar al-Sunna was another important insurgent group, primarily made up of Sunni Kurds, determined to establish an Islamic law state governed by Sharia.[28]

---

28 See, Ansal al-Islam, Mapping Militant Organizations, retrieved on 20 March, 2015. http:// web.stanford.edu/group/ mappingmilitants/cgi-bin/groups/view/13?highlight=ansar+al-islam. Ansar al-Sunna later became Ansar al-Islam.

The proceedings of these groups were dwarfed by Zarqawi with his range of attacks to gain publicity. Zarqawi opened his account of death with a car bomb attack on the Jordanian embassy in Baghdad on 7th August 2003 killing at least a dozen people (ibid). Another on 18th August, a suicide cement truck loaded with high explosives into UN headquarters killed twenty people and injured another seventy (ibid). Sergio de Mello, the head of the UN mission in Iraq, survived the initial blast but died several hours later. Zarqawi needed to hit a big target to recruit followers.[29] With his regular attacks, Zarqawi's motives were clear. He wanted to gain publicity and targeted US missions and the Shia people and their shrines. On 29th August 2003, just ten days after his lethal attack on UN, Zarqawi struck the very heart of Shia Islam and killed one of its most senior religious leaders and politicians. Bakir al-Hakim was killed with a suicide bomber in the holy city of Najaf killing Hakim and ninety others (Peritz and Rosenbach, 2012). For Zarqawi this was a huge coup that had just started. On March 2nd 2004, Zarqawi's suicide bomber attacked Shias in Baghdad and the second holy city of Karbala. Such atrocities soon made Zarqawi a most wanted terrorist with a $25 million (Hosken, 2015) reward on offer from the US government.

On 17th October 2004, Zarqawi and his Tawid wa'l Jihad group issued an online statement of pledging bayat

---

29 See, *Sergio*, HBO Documentary, 2009.

with AQ and hence the group was renamed as Al-Qaeda in Iraq (AQI) (ibid). Despite his pledge of bayat, AQI continued to act independently of AQ and pursued a strategy sometimes at odd with Bin Laden's approach (Stern and Berger, 2015). Zarqawi's reign of atrocities had made an impression in Iraq, igniting a cascade of violence as he continued to focus on secretarian targets, over AQ Central's objectives. In February 2006, the al Askari mosque in Samarra was bombed by militants, resulting in severe damage to its structure. AQI did not claim credit for the attack but a captured member later confessed to orchestrating it. The attack was widely seen as precipitating a full-on civil war that threatened the entire nation, portending massive bloodshed to come (Knickmeyer in Ghosh, 2006).

Nada Bakos (CIA) was soon charged with tackling Zarqawi and his AQI down (Stren and Berger, 2015). After being appointed, the countermeasures soon followed to take down Zarqawi. Tackling Zarqawi down was a very difficult task; they used satellite phones which are much more difficult to track. Eventually hubris and cumulative intelligence cost Zarqawi his life in June 2006; the videotape that had been viral months before was used to track Zarqawi (Hosken, 2015). In June 2006, the effort of Bakos and others were realised after Zarqawi was killed in an air strike. Soon after the fall of Zarqawi, Nouri al Maliki who had formed a new government of Iraq with US support declared about Zarqawi's demise in a conference. Zarqawi was dead but he had already made important structural changes by incorporating other jihadi groups making his organisation that covered enormous geographical space in Iraq (ibid).

Soon after the fall of Zarqawi, Abu Omar Al-Baghdadi succeeded. Omar followed the legacy of Zarqawi by targeting Shias and takfirs. After the death of Zarqawi, Zawahiri had issued a statement saying that AQ was not responsible for atrocities created by AQI. AQI had operated independently under Zarqawi. Omar took this to the next level of autonomy by announcing the establishment of the Islamic State of Iraq (ISI).[30]Maliki supported De-bathification policy and he was suspicious on ISI magnetisation of Sunni fighters. Such disfranchisement towards Sunnis marginalised them from various districts creating a more hostile situation in the country. His inclination towards Tehran brewed offensive Shia exploitation against the Sunnis creating an ambiguous situation in the country between Shias and Sunnis.

Abu Omar Al-Baghdadi had to act in order to shield people from Maliki's hostile policies so he called upon officers of the former Iraqi army who had victims of De-bathification policy. His appeal to Saddam's former

---

30   Although the organization was named as Islamic State of Iraq, the word State may be misleading. It is not used in the modern sense of Nation-State with territorial boundaries, but in an earlier sense that reflects the idea of the Caliphate and Islamic Space not delineated by defined geographical boundaries.

officers would reap long-term rewards; they would join ISI and help turn in into the more effective military machine. ISI already knew their worth. Many former soldiers and security officials had already joined ISI along with the Jihadis in US prison camps. After recruiting the sufficient number of former military personnel and soldiers, Omar announced his new cabinet for ISI. There would be ten ministries to govern the Anbar towns and territories, just the beginning of a new caliphate including one for public relations. With no hint of irony, a Professor named Janabi would be public security while the ministry of martyrs and prisoner affairs went to minor tribal sheikh whose main income came from smuggling (Kazimi, 2015).

ISI as an ANSA with such an organised system and mechanism carried out its violent activities as never before. Towards the end of 2006, an authoritative survey published by the *Lancet,* the prestigious U.K.-based medical journal, estimated that more than 600,000 people (Hosken, 2015) had been killed in Iraq since the start of US-led invasion. Omar had destroyed law and order by attacking policemen in the areas under their control. Policemen were threatened and they resigned or ISI. In Anbar province, ISI detonated a petrol tank outside a police station, killing everybody inside. Whoever survived was thrown in the river Euphrates with rocks tied to their legs (ibid). In places where ISI had control, Sharia laws were imposed. Bank robberies were common. In Ramadi, ISI issued fatwas closing factories, schools and universities that were European in nature (ibid).

By March 2007, ISI had launched chemical warfare on Sunni cities and to people who were reluctant in joining hands with ISI. Fighters number was on the rise once Omar had taken. Of the fighters that listed their nationality, 41% were from Saudi Arabia (Fishman, 2008), with Libya as the next most represented country. Syria, Yemen and Algeria made up 19.2% (ibid). The vast majority of recruits were in the twenties with some as young as sixteen (ibid). As a result of ISI's propaganda and its control over fighters, 14th August marked a dark period of government efficiency in combating ANSA. ISI suicide bombers attacked the villages of Qataniya and Adnaniya in Kurd controlled North-West Iraq on the Syrian border. Four ISI suicide bombers used three cars and a petrol tanker packed with a total of around two tons of explosives (Hosken, 2015). At least 500 people (ibid) were killed and another 375 injured (ibid) in the blasts, which levelled whole swathes of the two villages, leaving entire families buried under the rubble (ibid). It was the second hazardous attack since 9/11.

Prior to these attacks, the US launched Operation Phantom Phoenix to destabilise and defeat ISI. The US also took help from the insurgent groups like The Awakening to defeat ISI. Their combined operation began to greatly diminish ISI hold in Iraq. In response to this operation, ISI used women with Down Syndrome as human bombs so that it would go unnoticed and carrying out their operation would be easy. However, Prime Minister Maliki started a crackdown against Sunni insurgent *"The Awakening"* which further strengthened ISI stronghold at Anbar. The US still carried out their operation and it was successful in April 2010 when Omar and Masri were killed in an air strike led by the US. Soon after their death, Maliki produced photographs of both Masri and Omar corpse to end the speculation about their death. Soon after the death of ISI figure, the US concluded its mission in Iraq withdrawing its sphere of influence in the region. So why didn't the US finish off ISI when it was so clearly on its last legs? As James Franklin Jeffrey, the US ambassador to Iraq for almost two years stated that they were doing whatever they could to finish off ISI when Omar was dead. But it had been very difficult for them because of the usage of human bombs against them and ISI still had control over all kind of Transnational Criminal Organisations to raise funds. As the US had already withdrawn its troops from Iraq under the Obama Administration and misadventure among the US and Iraqi government did not allow plans to materialise into reality. The budget was also poorly allocated to continue to counter ANSA like ISI in Iraq. ISI had been pushed to the edge of oblivion but not into it (Hosken, 2015).

Following the death of Omar Al-Baghdadi, Abu Bakr Al-Qurayshi al-Husseini Al-Baghdadi was named as a leader of ISI. His first priority after becoming a leader was his own personal safety. With ISI in shambles, Baghdadi set out to rebuild the organisation eliminating potential critics and replacing them with trusted allies, many of whom had spent several years with Baghdadi in Camp Bucca.[31] Al-Baghdadi made significant changes in ISI and engulfed a major portion of Iraq and Syria. At first, no one knew much about Baghdadi. It was only after he was declared the leader of ISI people started to scan him in detail with his background. Although there are many speculations about his real name, it is believed that his real name was Ibrahim Awad Ibrahim al-Badri. Born in 1971, he was from a very religious family and his father was an Imam in a mosque. Having a religious background, he earned his Bachelor's and Master's degrees at Baghdad University where he studies Islamic Law and Koran and PhD in Islamic Studies. He would later put his knowledge to an effect in controlling ISI (ibid).

In early adulthood, Baghdadi was the member of the Iraqi branch of the Muslim Brotherhood.[32] The future caliph disagreed with the Brotherhood's strategy for how to bring about an Islamic Empire because they were reluctant in using force to serve their desire later so Baghdadi was against such strategy because he believed that only force would help them to establish Islamic Caliphate. What is puzzling about Baghdadi is that after the invasion he did not join Zarwqawi, instead he set up a small ANSA with Islamic ideological base named Abid

---

31 Camp Bucca was the principal detention facility run by the US in Southern Iraq for the bulk of the Iraqi extremist insurgents captured in the five previous years.

32 Mainstream Transnational ANSA with Islamic base that wants to bring about Caliphate.

Humam al-Athari (Army of the Sunni people) which was small and relatively unknown ANSA (ibid).

Baghdadi was arrested on 4 February 2004 in Fallujah and was jailed at Camp Bucca in Compound 6, which was characterised as a medium security Sunni compound. It was here he met many of the Ba'athist army officers who would help him strengthen ISI. In Camp Bucca, Baghdadi was tortured and humiliated which made him hate the Americans. Camp Bucca processed 100,000 (ibid) suspected Sunni insurgents in the five years of its operation and became known as a terrorist university. The US had accidentally created the next Islamic fundamentalist class where the detainees were introduced to various thinkers and activist like Qutb, Bin Laden, Ibn Wahhab et al. Eventually, in December 2004, he was released and at the end of January 2006, he joined Zarqawi's group (ibid). By all accounts, Baghdadi rose quickly through the Mujahedeen Shura Council, becoming a member of the organisation's Majalis al-Shura Council, its main political and decision-making body. Following the declaration of ISI, he also became General Supervisor of the Sharia Committees, putting a test to his Islamic Knowledge (ibid).

The source known as Wikibaghdady asserts that the former Ba'athist intelligence brigadier Haji Bakr acted as a kingmaker for Baghdadi in the days following the deaths of Omar and others. Haji Bakr soon became Baghdadi's right hand and probably his most important strategist

(Reuter, 2015). Soon after Baghdadi took over, he sent six suicide bombers to attack the heavily fortified Church on Iraqi Christian minorities. It killed fifty-eight (Shadid, 2010) people including policemen. This attack was seen as a strike at Iraq's core. After this attack, crackdown followed on Baghdadi and US state department offered for $10 million (ibid) reward for informing about his hideouts and whereabouts. But he could not be tracked because he had proper operational security and had learnt from his predecessor's mistakes (ibid).

ISI under Baghdadi's command was ruthless as ever committing genocide against minorities and unbelievers. He believed that jihad is the only way to reach Allah triggering an everlasting civil war in Iraq which later spread to other West Asian countries under Baghdadi's command. Osama Bin Laden was also killed by the US in Pakistan, the SEAL (Sea, Air and Land) team of the US accomplished the mission. Soon after Osama's death in 2011, Baghdadi warned that there would be a revenge for Osama's death and the US would pay for what they had done. While Iraq was in civil war busy trying to skirmish ISI, another significant event engulfed West Asian region and North Africa. Arab Spring or Arab Awakening which is often referred to as the fourth wave of democratisation became glare of publicity in IR.

The popular mobilisation of Arab Spring or Arab Awakening was driven by economic, social and political concerns of the people in the Arab World to take to the streets to demand reform of their leaders and even a change of power. The authoritarian resilience by which states like Tunisia, Libya and Yemen had been characterised appeared to crumble in the face of popular rebellion (Lynch, 2013). The rebellion appeared to have seismic in scale and potential for political change in the region that gave rise to jihadi/salafi interpretation and ANSA. Hence, the roots of Arab Awakening are extremely complex – strategically, geographically, evolving economic, national, ethnic and violent forces. In sum, the Arab Awakening is a long cycle of upheaval and instability that will probably take a decade to understand (Beverley, 2013).

Arab Awakening witnessed more complex and dynamic role played by a variety of organisations, groups and armed actors usually residing within jihadi/salafi interpretation. Radical Islamic interpretation had their part in the unfolding events but was not centre stage. Indeed, the call for democracy, constitutional rule and multi-party elections heard in the demands of demonstrators, young and old alike, was and remains markedly dissimilar from radical Islamic agendas commonly associated with the politics of West Asia. But it does not mean that there was a wholesale rejection of radical Islamic discourses. The Arab Awakening forced radical Islamic discourses to emerge and compete in a dynamic transnational landscape. The Awakening gave rise to Muslim protestors who joined with other social forces, groups and ANSA (ibid).

The Arab Awakening took place in the name of freedom and democracy, not jihad. Nevertheless, ANSA epitomised by radical Islamic interpretation filled in the political vacuum of fragile countries. In conflict, ANSAs attempted to break the hegemonic control of the state and its influence over the institutions of Islam. Muslim states elites acting as proxies of the West were portrayed as the near enemy in jihadi propaganda and became the target of their violent calls (ibid).

The onset of Arab Awakening witnessed the proliferation of ANSAs in West Asia, matched by the consequent increase in their significance for political dynamics across the region (Durac, 2015). It includes an array of Islamist actors and ANSAs epitomised by the jihadi/salafi school. For instance, in Yemen, after Ali Abdullah Saleh stepped down, Yemeni politics witnessed the rise of ANSAs like Houthi rebels and AQAP. The country became vulnerable with the civil war where AQAP and Houthi rebels compete to capture provinces breaking the country apart. In Libya, the anti-Gaddafi movement was joined by tribal groups, Islamists and others. This cross-ideological coalition, together with small ANSAs spelt the end of the Gaddafi era in Libyan political life. The fall of Gaddafi witnessed the rise of ANSAs in Zintan, Tripoli, Misrata and Benghazi (ibid) and those forming an alliance to counter western influence in the country. In Tunisia, Islamist actors played a significant role where Islamist Nadha Party won the election after Ben Ali stepped down (Gasiorowski, 2014).Similarly, the fall of

Hosni Mubarak in Egypt galvanised the participation of ANSAs in the political sphere of the country. ANSAs like Muslim Brotherhood formed an alliance to rule the country and elected Muhammad Morsi as a President (Lowe, 2013).

The proliferation of ANSAs during and after the Arab Awakening in West Asia is co-related with the growing weakness of many states in the region. States with a low level of legitimacy were unable to maintain the loyalty of many within their populations. When such states resort to repression, they typically provoke opposition. Similarly, when states exclude significant elements of their populations through neglect, lack of capacity or some other form of discrimination, they create conditions within which ANSAs emerge (Durac, 2015). The Arab Awakening witnessed these weaknesses of states where countries like Tunisia, Libya, Egypt, Yemen and others were affected. Undoubtedly, the greatest focus during the Arab Awakening and post period has been the rise ANSAs in Iraq and Syria.

In Syria and Iraq, a wave of democratic protests took of disastrously. Syria had been ruled by the Baathist regime since 1963 and the state of emergency imposed at that time was still in place. Serious uprisings began in March 2011 when some children were arrested and allegedly tortured for writing anti-government slogans in the southern city of Darra. Protests rapidly spread to Damascus, and to other cities of Homs. President Bashar al-Assad showed very little willingness to make concessions-security forces responded harshly and army tanks were used to suppress the revolt. Syrians who were subjected to decades of family dictatorship regime were inspired by the events in the Arab World and started their anti-Assad protest in the hope of toppling Assad. The protest began at Deraa where seventy-two people (Berger and Stern, 2015) were killed by the security forces. People continued with spray painting in the town of Deraa against Assad's authoritarian rule where fifteen demonstrators were arrested and tortured brutally. The mob started reacting to this vicious act as a result the government responded with ferocity which led to officers defect from the army and join the rebel groups fighting the regime. The protest became global in social networking sites like Facebook and Twitter (Hosken, 2015).

Assad ended state of emergency but still the protest continued. It was on May 28th 2011 the body of a thirteen-year-old boy was delivered to his family and the child's genitalia had been removed resulting in a widespread protest where it was suppressed by guns and chemical weapons. (Berger and Stern, 2015) This reached the international level and alerted the UN permanent members, that Assad was using chemical weapons to suppress the revolt, the member countries of the UN wanted to topple Assad out of power to bring in stability in the region which had been highly concentrated with the rebel groups wanting to throw Assad out of power but Russia and China vetoed it.

In this predicament NATO countries like U.K., France alongside US and Gulf Countries led by Saudi Arabia funded the rebels so that Assad would be toppled but things turned out to be poles apart. The Awakening in Syria gave rise to Muslim protestors who joined with other social groups and organisations to call for freedom, dignity and equality but this led to the brewing of radical Islamic interpretation in social bodies. When countries like Saudi and other Gulf states were inclined to bring in Sunni regime in Syria, Iran on the other hand provided support for Assad. Since Iran and Saudi had been involved in a proxy war for decades, the regional bipolar rivalry was seen in Syria's case where one party supported Assad and others wanted to topple it.

At this time, Baghdadi had been operating in Iraq and was fighting Maliki's hostile policies against Sunni people. Maliki's policy against Sunni people magnetised Baghdadi's recruitment. Iraq had been in turmoil even before the Arab Spring under Maliki's rule. Maliki suspected all Sunnis of being jihadist. He also tried to arrest top Iraqiya Sunni leaders. Strategically this proved a disastrous move and played a significant part in the resurgence of Baghdadi and his group. Maliki sent troops and tanks to surround the homes of Sunni people. Widespread Sunni protests took place throughout The Awakening period and he was convinced that Baghdadi was involved in the growing mayhem that had swept the whole region (Hosken, 2015).

In mid-2011, as Syria descended rapidly from public protests-violently suppressed-into all-out civil war, Baghdadi dispatched a tiny team of Jihadis across the border that had been porous since US invasion in Iraq. Baghdadi instructed Jihadis to fight against Assad. Heading the team was young Syrian Jihadi Abu Muhammad al-Jawlini who established a group of fighters and named them as Al-Nusra Ash-Sham (ibid). They first came to prominence in the civil war in Syria with a series of hazardous suicide bombings. With Jawlini's experience of fighting alongside ISIS in Iraq, he moulded his Nusra in and quickly rose to prominence among the hundreds of militia leaders then battling Assad. Unlike ISI, Nusra had been partially successful in portraying a humanitarian face to many Syrian people carrying out polio vaccination programmes. Among the estimated 1,600 (ibid) and more rebel groups in Syria, Nusra was most effective in carrying out high-profile and high-casualty attacks. It also did something that Baghdadi and ISI would carve for it, it took territory. When the Gulf states and NATO funded these ANSAs with weapons and other aid to throw Bashar out of power, things turned out to be different (Stern and Berger, 2015). These ANSAs became independent and carried out their operations themselves. Soon weapons went into the hands of these independent ANSAs which also included Al-Nusra. Nusra soon started taking territories. Raqqa was captured and on hearing this, Baghdadi decided to travel Syria and bring Nusra back under his personal control. To do this, he planned to dissolve both ISI and Nusra, merge the two ANSA and declare ISIS (Islamic State of Iraq and Syria) (Hosken, 2015).

However, Nusra did not approve of this merger plan. Even AQ, now under Zawahiri did not approve the ISI merger plan. Still ISI had already renamed itself as ISIS and carried out their operation widely. The two groups came to direct confrontation giving way to *"war within a war"* (Berger and Stern, 2015) where ISIS/ISIL was now battling with other rebel groups including Al-Nusra. Al-Qaeda leader Zawahiri gave in writing *"ISIS is not a branch of Al-Qaeda group and we have no organisational relationship with it, and Al-Qaeda is not responsible for its action"*(ibid;33–53). This is a clear indication that ISIS was not willing to share power with other Armed Non-State Actors and acted independently. The members of other small ANSAs operating in Iraq and Syria joined ISIS since they could vision future with ISIS and they had been marginalised by Maliki's regime in Iraq and Assad in Syria. Due to lack of opportunity and poverty Sunni population from the tribal villages thought it better to join hands with ISIS. With the strength, ISIS overran the town of Azaz in 2013. By 2014 ISIS took the city of Raqqa from Al-Nusra and established its capital there. Tikrit, Baiji, Saqlawiyah, Fallujah towns of Rawa, Ana, Huseiba and Rutba were also taken which falls under Syrian province. They also took over the city of Deir ez Zour from Al-Nusra, Qaraqosh, Yazadi city of Sinjar was also taken under control by the regime (Dhiman, 2015).

ISIS starting from 2013 made vast military gains capturing major portions in Iraq and Syria fighting series of warfare with the regimes and other rebel groups who are funded by the West to fight ISIS. It was in September 2013 ISIS captured Azaz, and by December ISIS had over ran the cities of Aleppo, Maskana and Ashrar ash – Sham fighting with the other rebel groups like Al – Nusra, Free Syrian Army and Kurdish forces in the region. In 2014 ISIS took over other territories in the region. In early June ISIS seized control over Mosul, Falluja and Tikrit. The fall of Mosul was a severe blow to Iraq as it took the second largest populated city in Iraq and because of its strategic location, it is a cross-border of Iraq and Syria and from Mosul ISIS succeeded in its operation capturing other provinces and bringing under their control. They also captured the Iraqi city of Tal Afar. On June 22nd ISIS ran over Al-Quaim and from there ISIS could now transport war machines and their Islamic Army in Iraq and Syria and the region is rich in oil reserves which boosted the financial network of ISIS. In August, ISIS fighters took the city of Zumbar and Quaraqosh battling with the Kurdish forces in the north. By 13th August ISIS had taken over the city of Aleppo not far from Turkey border. (ibid)

ISIS succeeded in capturing many cities in Iraq and Syria and later when ISIS had transpired into a powerful ANSA it was too late for the U.S to react. However, they changed their focus from toppling the Assad regime to fight the ISIS. ISIS became a common enemy of the rivals who was grumbling over the issue of failure of the Arab Spring in West Asia mainly Syria. Initially, the intervention of foreign forces was not present but the funding was done to fight the organisation alongside Assad. It was realised in June 29th 2014 when ISIS captured a number of Iraqi and Syrian cities and declared caliph and establishment of Islamic State all over West Asia and beyond, the plague of ISIS was realised (Hosken, 2015).

In Iraq, ISIS had taken control over Tikrit, Baiji, Qaim, Rutba, Anah, Ramadi, Falluja, Tal Afar, Haditha Dam, Mosul, Samarra, Anbar, Kirkuk, Erbil and other territories. *In Syria* ISIS took control over the cities held by Al-Nusra and other rebel group as war within war emerged, at first when the situation was ripe for ISIS to expand they took Dier Al Zour and later ISIS took the cities of Raqqa, Aleppo, Hama, Homs, Palmyra and other Sunni villages in the region. (Berger and Stern, 2015) With this it is clear that ISIS has taken over massive land in Iraq and Syria which has become a concern for the West as it challenges their interest in the region. ISIS emerged as a potent Armed Non-State Actor in West Asia occupying landmass big as the United Kingdom (Hosken, 2015).

The rampant expansion of ISIS as an armed Non-State Actor gained more glare of publicity in the international arena. It was on 29th June 2014 when Abu Bakr Al-Baghdadi was declared as a new Caliph Ibrahim at Mosque in Mosul. ISIS claims to establish an Islamic

State and called out to Muslims all over the world for Hijrah and fight against the takfirs and join help ISIS for Global Jihad (ibid). This sent a wave of fear among the countries in West Asia and Western countries. ISIS as an ANSA came to spotlight driven by Islamic ideological base.

2.5 Conclusion

It is apparent that transnational links of Islam have created a different interpretation that has now become an ideological base of ANSAs. ANSAs like AQ, Hezbollah, Boko Harem etc. have wielded Islam as an ideological base. Following 9/11 attacks, western status has changed towards ANSAs driven by radical Islamic ideological base. The change of their status was seen during the invasion of Iraq that created a power vacuum in the country that helped various ANSAs to operate in Iraq with such ideological base.

However, the historical evolution of ISIS was seen since the Soviet intervention of Afghanistan when AQ expanded its bodies to various countries. The rise of ISIS have deep roots since the invasion of Iraq where Zarqawi was let free to operate. Above all, the Arab Awakening triggered the rise of ISIS where ANSAs epitomised by Islamic fundamentalism took an active part in the demonstration and political transition. It was the political instability in Iraq and Syria and western powers including regional superpowers involvement and their ambiguity that led to the grown of ISIS from the crisis. ISIS has now become a global concern for the globe because of its growing influence and attacks that they carry out. ISIS has given new definition to ANSAs with its manipulation and evolution within ANSAs in contemporary world politics.

Chapter III

Structure and *Modus Operandi* of ISIS

3.1 Introduction

ISIS is not only shaped by the leader and his background, the group's demographic and possible internal hierarchical system or context within which it operates. ISIS operates with complete unity of effort, ideology, motivations and interests from top to bottom. Internal and external characteristics of ISIS are interdependent with each other. ISIS's structure and modus operandi provide a set of possible external supports from other ANSAs. When ISI transpired into ISIS, the group's structure and modus operandi also went through the transformational phase where it has now become the most well organised ANSA.

This chapter will comprehend the structure and modus operandi of ISIS while focusing on its recruitment strategies that has magnetised fighters to join ISIS, affiliation with other groups where groups like Boko Harem etc. have pledged an alliance with ISIS, financial mechanisms, weapons that they use against their enemies, the way they administer the conquered provinces and how they implement Islamic jurisprudence. Furthermore, this chapter also focuses on how internal and external characteristics of ISIS and how it has helped them become the most formidable ANSAs and an evolution post 9/11 period.

3.2 ISIS Organisational Structure

ISIS has controlled a major portion in Iraq and Syria over the years using their method of manipulation control mechanisms. An ANSA organising such a massive area of 243,000 (Stern and Berger, 2015) square kilometre and establishing a de-facto state in the dominated region is quite an impossible task if the organisation is not systematised. ISIS is properly systematised unlike other ANSA. It is because of responsibility that ISIS has promised to re-establish the Islamic jurisprudence all across the region which they have claimed under their control as an Islamic Caliphate and maintain Ummah. It is lucid that ISI was transpired into ISIS. When ISI was being conversed, its governance hierarchy and responsibility also went through the process of transformation which has facilitated the organisation to control the incarcerated region effortlessly to maintain Ummah and preserve the proclamation of the caliph and Islamic State.

ISIS uses strict hierarchy system to operate their planning and missions. Abu Bakr Al-Baghdadi is the leader of ISIS who is a self-appointed caliph, he is known as Caliph Ibrahim al-Qureshi to his followers. There are two deputy positions under Abu Bakr, one is for Syria and the other for Iraq. Deputy Emir of Syria is Abu Ali al-Anbari.[33] Emir of Syria looks after provinces in Syria that are incarcerated by ISIS. Provinces in Syria include Aleppo, Al-Hasakah, Dimashq, Gezira, Hama, Homs, Dier Ez-Zor and Ar-Raqqa.[34] Deputy/ Emir of Iraq is Turkmani. Deputy/Emir of Iraq looks after provinces like Anbar, Tigris, Diyala, Euphrates, Fallujah, Gezira, Junoub, Kirkuk, Ninevah, North Baghdad and Salahuddin. Emir of Iraq and Syria also looks after provinces targeted by ISIS. They appoint commanders and send fighters to counter state forces and also to defend their foothold. Kobane can be taken as an example here. ISIS had initially captured Kobane from Kurdish forces however they were pushed downward with a coalition that fought against ISIS. Kobane is now a stronghold of YPG (Nance, 2016).

There are thirteen Governors (Lister, 2015) under Syria and Iraq, each making 24 (Nance, 2016) who fills in the council of the organisation. There are seven (ibid) councils and each has their own powers and responsibilities making ISIS as a formidable ANSA. Financial council: responsible for weapons, oil sale and

---

33 Deputies keep changing. Anbari was reportedly killed on December 12, 2015. Present Deputy of Syria is unknown. For a better understanding Anbari will be used to analyse Deputy's position.

34 It is to be noted that provinces keep shifting from State to ISIS because of ongoing battle between ISIS and coalition fighting to skirmish ISIS.

revenue of acquired territories (Lister, 2015). Leadership Council: makes law and major policies (ibid). Military Council: military decisions and advancement in the region. Fighter's assistance council: manages foreign and local fighters (Nance, 2016). Security Council: makes internal policies. Intelligence Council: gives information on advancing rebels and regimes in neighbouring areas and find out places where an attack could be easily made (ibid). Media council: controls social media (ibid). ISIS also has a cabinet of advisers where they advise on general management officials; prisoners and detainees; general security; general finance; general coordinator between Islamic State's provinces; general jihadi management and general military council (Nance, 2016). This cabinet of advisers is headed by a cabinet which takes charge of each cabinet. ISIS also has a Shura council, they are consultants on military and religious concerns (Lister, 2015). They also have the power to appoint another caliph challenging the power of Al-Baghdadi. Shura consists of seven members (Nance, 2016) and they are; Amari. Turkmani, Anbari, Shishani, Ayman, Al-Absi and Al-Adnani. Shura follows strict Islamic jurisprudence and makes sure that everyone goes by law and order featured by them (ibid).

3.3 Recruitment

ISIS has magnetised fighters and believers from three factors; external intervention, Arab Revolts and Social

Jihad (Stern and Berger, 2015). External Intervention: After the collapse of the government of Saddam Hussain by the U.S, members of Bathist party who were loyal to Saddam regime were banned from the Iraqi politics leaving them unemployed. When ISIS emerged the majority of the Sunni members of Bathist party joined the ISIS which included former military generals, soldiers, strategy thinkers and others increasing the number of fighters.

Arab Revolts: The wave of democracy protests began in Arab countries which challenged the authoritarian regimes. In Syria, Assad used chemical weapons to suppress the Sunni uprising and in Iraq Maliki targeted the Sunni people and attacked Sunni villages making them homeless. These hostile policies adopted by Maliki and Assad added fuel to the fire making the region more vulnerable, when ISIS was formed these oppressed people joined the group as they were left with no option.

Social Jihad: when Al-Baghdadi claimed to establish the Islamic State in and around West Asia, Muslim people who were unemployed and deprived of basic human rights in other countries saw this as an opportunity for Hijrah and Global Jihad. This led to widespread recruitment across the world. After jihad went Social on Facebook, Yahoo, Gmail and Twitter more fighters joined ISIS (ibid). Social Jihad is a new brainchild which ISIS has pieced and it cost nothing to email on social networking cite and publish videos on YouTube (ibid).

It was during the Arab Spring that revolution was tweeted with hash tags (#) it became influential to Armed Non-State Actors and the usage became widespread. ISIS became the first jihadist group to use social networking site like Twitter to spread their sphere of influence across the world, they set up their first official Twitter account named *al I'tisaamm* formed in October 2013 and it quickly gained 24,000 (ibid) followers.

ISIS has created 50,000[35] official Twitter accounts across the globe and these accounts have been extensively used for recruitment policy. From Europe ISIS recruited 17,000[36] to 19,000[37] fighters. Majority of its fighters were from Africa and West Asia who travelled all the way to Iraq and Syria for *Hijrah* and fight alongside the jihadist group. In October 2013, Radio Free Europe and Radio Liberty estimated more fighters were joining the organisation drawn from various other sources. Tunisia and Saudi Arabia contributed the majority of foreign fighters (Stern and Berger, 2015), Tunisia alone contributed 3,000[38] fighters who have already joined the organisation. ISIS has become a global armed Non-State Actor recruiting 70,000[39]

---

35 See, *Economist*. 2015. Islamic State: The propaganda war. August 15, pp 41-42.

36 ibid.

37 ibid.

38 ibid.

39 ibid.

fighters including 15,000–20,000[40] foreign fighters who are employed to strike in different countries.[41] The fighters are paid $400 (ibid) per month and it increases on the basis of seniority.

ISIS was looking for volunteers to raise fund and expansion process and also people who could work with sophisticated technology. They required scholars, doctors, engineers, professionals and others who could expand the legitimacy and build a strong potent force of armed Non-State Actor indulged in all dimension of globalisation. In this regard, Abu Bakr Al-Baghdadi says:

> *"We make a special call to soldiers,(Islamic legal experts), especially the judges, as well as people with military, administrative and service expertise, medical doctors, engineers of all various specialisation and fields"* (ibid; 86).

This clearly shows that ISIS was recruiting people who were willing to join voluntarily. Social jihad did magnetise fighters to join hands with ISIS in Global Jihad. There is no exact headcount as to how many fighters are in ISIS (Nance, 2016). From Canada, officials place the number of fighters at 130 (Amanda, 2015). From the US, FBI Director said unofficial 250 and more have travelled to Syria and Iraq (US Homeland Security Committee, 2015). From Europe total of 4654 fighters have joined ISIS out

---

40 ibid.

41 ibid.

of which 1700 (Nance, 2016) are from France making it the highest contributor to ISIS forces.[42] Contributing countries from Western Europe are Austria, Belgium, Britain, Denmark, France, Finland, Germany, Ireland, Italy, Netherland, Norway, Portugal, Spain, Sweden and Switzerland. From the Balkans (Albania, Bosnia, Kosovo and Serbia) 687 (ibid) fighters have joined ISIS. From Russia and Eastern Europe, 2798 (ibid) fighters have joined ISIS From Central Asia, 2096 (ibid) fighters: from Sub-Saharan Africa 173 (ibid): from East and Southeast Asia, 1895 (ibid) fighters; From Oceania 126 (ibid) fighters.

Looking at the magnitude of foreigners willingness to join ISIS by performing Hijrah has dwarfed other ANSAs and radical Islamic ANSAs. This is something that sets ISIS apart from other ANSAs. They have been the first radical Islamic ANSAs to use social media to magnetise fighters as a momentous element of their recruitment stratagem. To comprehend ISIS recruitment stratagem, one must look at who they target. Majority of the suppressed Sunni population in Iraq and Syria strengthened the foothold of ISIS. In majority of their foreign recruits there is no specific socio-economic, educational or religious common background or upbringing found in their recruits; however, they target the weak, the lonely and those who feel like they have nothing to lose in the life

---

42 These figures from Europe are unofficial estimation made by government authorities.

they are living, and provide them with a new life that promises to be better than anything they might have at home. The most potential recruits might enjoy good life but most do not feel committed to lives they are living. This is the point where Jihadism steps in, to fill the void that their life is causing. Loneliness is the most important factor that can get a person to leave ISIS (Rukmini, 2015).[43]

Loneliness is not the only reason to be victimised by ISIS recruitment strategy. In 2014, Asher Abid Khan, nineteen at that time of his recruitment, made the trip to Turkey before deciding to go back home. He was persuaded by the propaganda of ISIS that continuously posted in social networking site. According to his lawyer,

> *"decided he should do something to help his brothers and sisters in Islam… The ideas being sent out are sophisticated in the sense that they portray a romantic ideal of something, in the nature of a religious obligation or duty in jihad"* (Dorian, 2015; 1).

---

43 This was the case of Alex, a 23 year old women living with her grandparents in a small town in the US. She gave an interview to The New York Times, describing her close relationship with ISIS fighters. While communicating with ISIS, they provided her with hours of deep conversation about spirituality, religion and politics; but were also there when she needed someone to speak with and demoralized her about the life she was living. She later converted to Islam.

Young youths who lack a clear sagacity of what they want in their lives may be magnetised towards an idea to brawl for something gigantic than things they could encounter in their daily lives or job. Ideas such as the fight for Muslim community have magnetised more travellers in the recruitment process of ISIS (ibid).

For the young men it is clear that their dream of becoming a hero can be actualised by ISIS but for women the scenario is different. Why would they leave everything behind and join ISIS where they have been exploited or treated as a third class in ISIS hierarchy? To understand such mystification, a French Journalist named Anna Erelle creates a fake account in social networking site naming herself as Melodie. She wanted to find out the recruitment networks of ISIS and how teen girls are carried away by the jihadist group. She let herself be recruited by a man called Bilel, under the pseudonym Melodie. She portrayed her avatar Melodie as a sensitive young girl. Melodie was promised true love, marriage and an idyllic life in less than 48 hours after first establishing personal online contact with Bilel (member of ISIS). Her life was a desert and he was an oasis. Melodie already saw him as a king. And she had always dreamed of being a queen (Erelle, 2015).

Melodie was promised a flat like a palace and a husband who would take care of her all the time. Bilel mentioned that the life she was living in Paris is against Allah and whoever lives under the influence of capitalist state would be destroyed eventually and Sharia law will be established all across the globe (ibid). The recruitment network of ISIS is a vast sphere where various fighters in the group are involved in recruiting and brainwashing young men and women to join ISIS. A fighter named Omar Omsen who was wanted by both the French and Belgian police was thought to be one of the brains behind an important jihadist recruitment network that sent people from Europe to Middle East (ibid). Omar had organised their journey. He often posts videos on YouTube of himself praising Sharia law, encouraging viewers to ignore the laws of their countries and uphold only Islamic Sharia law (ibid). He tries to brainwash and shame them, saying things like

> *"A good Muslim doesn't live in a country of non-believers. If you aren't helping the Islamic State, then you're murderers. While you say your prayers and pore over the Koran, others are fighting for the one and only Allah, who wants us to establish a worldwide caliphate"* (ibid; 64).

Similarly, Melodie was also brainwashed by Bilel and he had asked her to travel to Germany at first and then dispose of her phone and sim card there in Germany and get a new one. Again she was asked to travel towards Turkey and dispose of the gadgets she had bought in Germany and contact Bilel and travel south towards rebel-held territories where a recruiter would come and pick her up and travel Syria. After entering Syria it would be easy for the ISIS fighters to take the vulnerable recruited men and women to Iraq. This was how it happened when a French citizen travelled for Hijrah. Melodie had a long conversation with Bilel where he disclosed that fighters from Iraq would be taken to Syria from Diez ez-Zor through a tunnel after coming to an agreement with rebels from Syria who controlled territories there (ibid). This was how the whole recruitment was taking place for Europeans especially.

As one has seen examples of fighters recruited by ISIS, the jihadi group is operated by experts in the recruitment process. They promise the vulnerable people of what they want in their life. They are guaranteed a closeness of people in the community for loners; religious utopia for those looking for their purpose in life, a sense of moral superiority for those who are not completely convinced that they want to leave their life in the West; a promise of a heroic life full of victories for the greater good of the Ummah.[44] While recruiting members, one of the most common ground on convincing someone is by promising them that Sharia law would be established heavily criticising western model calling them corrupt and objectifying women for pleasure. They argue that *"women in Europe are treated badly and used as objects. Men show off like trophies"* (Erelle, 2015; 55), while assuring

---

44 See, Ristori, nd. Online Jihad: ISIS's Foreign Recruitment Strategies. Retrieved, 13th October, 2017, at: https://www.cmu.edu/dietrich/globalstudies/images/docs/cristina-martin-79-400-paper-s16.pdf.

the vulnerable and potential recruits that "*if they continue to live among kafirs, they will burn in hell*" (ibid; 33).

ISIS publication and their online videos have become a mobilising force for recruitment. In videos released by al-Hayat Media Centre, such as No Respite, is one of the stalwart propaganda of ISIS.[45] In this, they have used the concept of moral and religious superiority to magnetise recruits who will be inclined towards spirituality, adding up us versus them binary which will detract them from the western model.[46] They brag about how ISIS is committed to Sharia and will establish a caliphate. Throughout the visual content of that video, ISIS constantly give reference to multi-culturalism Islam and glory where the notion of nationalism has been abolished and come under a single Islamic jurisprudence.[47]

Similarly, in al-Hayat's video, Join the Ranks, potential recruits are asked by a jihadi "Are your homes, businesses, and wealth, more beloved to you than Allah, his messenger and jihad in his path?"[48] This brings a sense of belongings to the Islamic community for the viewers. The rise of Islamophobia and the catastrophic civilian deaths in Iraq and Afghanistan are constantly exploited

---

45   ibid.

46   ibid.

47   ibid.

48   Syria Focus. ""Join the ranks" from the Islamic State." *YouTubeVideo*, 8:27. Posted, July 2014. In. https://www.youtube.com/watch?v=kxsPR-_fYnk.

by ISIS to wage war against the West, and jihad is seen as the opportunity to fight for a greater cause than oneself, and to do something with your life that is incomparable to anything that can be done in the West. They sell loves in the west as futile, with statements like "*While we're out risking our lives, you're spending days doing meaningless activities. Being religious means imposing your values*" (ibid; 33). A jihadist promised Melodie, "*You'll have a little group of girlfriends, and you'll do girl stuff together*" (ibid; 75). While at the same time telling her "*you're my jewel, you're pure… You'll be really well taken care of here. You'll be important, And if you agree to marry me, I'll treat you like a queen*" (ibid; 52). It is lucid here that they promised marriage and happiness.

ISIS propaganda videos featured in the names, The Clanging of the swords part 1–4 (Stern and Berger, 2015) that showed the controlled territories of ISIS and how Sharia law was established. It also showed beheadings, stoning to death etc.. Another video that featured was, The management of Savagery(ibid) which also focused on ISIS greater propaganda. It highlighted the controlled territories but also mobilised youths in joining ISIS in the name of Hijrah. The tsunami of ISIS propaganda and recruitment continued where longer videos of good quality were released under the title, Flames of the War and The Resolve of the Defiant (Hosken, 2015) which visualised the execution of American citizen and other foreigners and minorities in ISIS-held territory.

Apart from the videos of beheadings, a significant force for mobilising youths and magnetisation of ISIS sympathisers increased with words from Adnani (spokesperson of ISIS). The conduct of *lone wolf attacks*[49] took off and people are performing Hijrah increased after the speech given by Adnani, directed to Islamic fighters. *Adnani* gave a speech to those who are living abroad and said,

> *"Mujahedeen in Europe, Australia and Canada… O mujahedeen in Morocco and Algeria… O mujahedeen in Khorasan, the Caucasus and Iran… O mujahedeen, we call you up to defend the Islamic State… So rise O mujahedeen. Rise and defend your state from your place wherever you may be."* He specified *"You must strike the soldiers, patrons and troops of the tawaghit*[50]. *Strike their police, security, and intelligence members, as well as their treacherous agents. Destroy their beds. Embitter their lives for them and make them busy with themselves. If you can kill a disbeliever American or European-especially the spiteful and filthy French – or an Australian or a Canadian, or any other disbeliever from the disbelieved waging war, including the citizens of the countries that entered into a coalition against the Islamic State, then rely upon Allah, and kill him in*

---

49 A lone wolf is someone who prepares and commits violent acts alone, outside of any command structure and without material assistance from any group. H/She may be influenced or motivated by the ideology and beliefs of an external group and may act in support of such a group.

50 Cross a limit or demarcation line.

any manner or way however it may be. Do not ask for anyone's advice and do not seek anyone's verdict. Kill the disbeliever whether he is civilian or military, for they have the same ruling. Both of them are disbelievers. Both of them are considered to be waging war (the civilian by belonging to a state waging war against the Muslims)" (Gambhir and Lewis, 2014; 1–2).

Adnani asked people who could join ISIS to perform Hijrah. For those who could not perform Hijrah were asked to attack the non-believers in their own soil (lone wolf attacks). For those who could not do both were asked to pledge bayat with ISIS. This statement made a big alteration strengthening foothold of ISIS.

3.4 Affiliates/Bayat

A serious challenge at any ANSAs might face is that of overstretch. In the case of ISIS, the movement is stretched vast, both territorially and ideologically (Aydinli, 2016). The connection of ISIS-affiliated ANSAs are growing stronger. ISIS network now incorporates a wide collection of people across the globe and groups sharing the same agenda of establishing the Islamic Caliphate. ISIS affiliation or bayat[51] has increased where various other ANSAs with radical Islamic ideological base pledged alliance with ISIS. As pointed out by Eisenhower, the

---

51 An oath of allegiance.

Domino Effect[52] has been actualised in understanding the expansion of ISIS which has deluded not only major portions in Iraq and Syria but has diversified its ideology beyond West Asia. Bayats have been established in the majority of the Muslim populated countries with ISIS where they have promised to fight for the caliphate and inaugurate Sharia law and Ummah there. ANSAs in countries like Lebanon, Egypt, Jordan etc. have pledged an alliance with ISIS. Circumstances in which other groups from these countries have pledged an alliance with ISIS is different. For a broader understanding of ISIS outstretch, one must look at these countries and their strong-weak continuum that has been exploited by ISIS and other groups.

3.4.1 Lebanon

As a corollary of long civil war in Lebanon and uncooked sentiments of the participants along religious lines, Lebanon's Shi'ite population backed Syrian President Assad in the 2011 Syrian Civil War (Nance, 2016). The Iranian-backed Lebanese Hezbollah became involved in the Syrian Civil War in 2013, on the side of the Syrian government (Alessandra, 2015). Hezbollah's involvement in Syria made Sunni elements there to retaliate against Hezbollah.

---

52 Domino effect or a chain reaction is the cumulative effect produced when one event sets off a chain of similar events. It was widely used during the Cold War to comprehend the expansion of Communist regime across the globe.

ISIS penetration in the country was seen in 2014 where the Lebanese border city of Tripoli and Arsal were featured with ISIS assaults (Nance, 2016). According to Major General Abbas Ibrahim, head of the Lebanese Directorate of General Security, ISIS troops infiltrated villages and areas around the Qalamon Mountains bordering Syria to obtain an advantageous position for fighting in Syria (ibid). An incursion and conquest of Lebanese is an ambition for ISIS, since Iranian government backing and the presence of Hezbollah would be solemnly an obstruction to their goal (ibid).

A severe blow to the Lebanese government and Hezbollah was seen in June 2014 when Free Sunnis of Baalbek (FSB) pledged alliance to the Islamic State via Twitter, they said;

> *"We announce our allegiance, with all pride, to the Mujahid Abu Bakr Al-Baghdadi as caliph of the Muslims... We also announce our full support for what (ISIS) is doing for Islam...it is the duty of all Muslims to work towards finding a caliph who can set up rule by Sharia law."*[53]

ISIS dream of establishing its hold in Lebanese soil was actualised by this oath of allegiance by this ANSA FSB. However, ISIS leadership has not been formally

---

53 Now. 2014. "Free Sunnis of Baalbeck Pledge Allegiance to ISIS Caliphate." *Now.* Accessed Dec.11, 2016: https://now.mmedia. me/lb/en/lebanonnews/553835-free-sunnis-of-baalbeck-pledge-allegiance-to-isis-caliphate.

recognised as a Lebanese affiliate. There is speculation that al-Maqdisi is the ISIS Emir of Lebanon (ibid).

3.4.2 Jordan

Jordan's government has been allied with the US for decades and its US-supplied military is strong and disciplined, making the kingdom a difficult military target for ISIS (Nance, 2016). In 2014, the Jordanian military repulsed a tentative incursion by ISIS forces into the kingdom. ISIS forces attempted to cross the border and seize the Turabil/Karame border post (Theodore, 2015). Although Jordan has a military alliance with the US, the population had a low opinion of the US and was internally susceptible to the ISIS message, until the burning death of a Jordanian pilot (David, 2015). ISIS has now stirred Jordanian outrage. Zarqa a poverty striven city north of Amman, remains a hotbed of unemployed young men and Islamic radicals (ibid).

On May 7, 2015, ISIS-affiliated Twitter account declared that Shahids Battalion of Ma'an in Jordan pledged allegiance to the caliph. Other customary video recordings of ISIS give subsequent acknowledgement by Al-Baghdadi, during which Al-Baghdadi announces leadership of the new group (Nance, 2016).

3.4.3 Gaza

The strip of Gaza has an extensive history of radical Islamic fundamentalism and its connection with ANSAs.

Numerous radical Islamic fundamentalists may be ISIS adherents but few have conducted Hijra to fight alongside ISIS. Hamas authorities have been quick to stamp out overt support for ISIS (Nance, 2016). ISIS operatives appear to play Hamas against Israel, especially by firing impotent rockets into Israeli territory. Whereas Hamas sees ISIS as a threat in Gaza, it may coordinate with ISIS in the Sinai Peninsula to traffic arms across the Egyptian border. In late 2015, the ISIS beheading of Hamas leader at the Yarmouth Palestinian refugee camp in Syria set off a tit-for-tat series of reprisals between ISIS and Hamas in Gaza (ibid).

The increasing number of assault against Hamas specifies that ISIS influence in Gaza has been increasing. This may pose a threat to Israel and Hamas both. Threat perception of Hamas and Israel was amplified when Mujahideen Shura Council in the Environs of Jerusalem issued a statement on February 2014 that they were committed to help ISIS and bolster its ranks. They (MSC) also believed that internal conflicts within the jihad in Syria were due to an unfair view towards ISIS and its emir Al-Baghdadi (Al-Ghoul, 2014). Ansar Beit al-Maqdis pledged alliance to ISIS in November 2014, changing its name to Sinai Province (Issacharoff, 2015). The sphere of influence that ISIS has left in Gaza made two groups to support ISIS.

ISIS in Gaza is the self-styled Gaza District of Islamic State. Little is known of senior membership;

Abu Qatadah al-Filistini appeared in a video calling on Gazans to join the covey of the mujahideen and to join the state of the Caliphate (Nance, 2016).

3.4.4 Egypt

In Egypt, the Arab Spring transformation was visualised. Many active ANSAs received very little oversight as the post-Mubarak power struggle ensued. After the fall of Mubarak, the government released prisoners, and these were mostly comprised of experienced fighters who went back to the pool. It was in 2011 after Jama'at al-Tawhid wal-Jihad (TWJ) joined with other small ANSAs, Ansar Beit al-Maqdis (ABM) was formed under the leadership of Tawfiq Mohammad Faraj. Faraj was executed in 2014 by Egyptian Authorities (ibid). Faraj was one holding smaller ANSA into one concrete TWJ (ibid).

When TWJ lost its leader, there was no one who could replace him. It seemed like TWJ crackdown by the authorities would end its superiority over other groups. In order to retain the position of TWJ and to maintain Islamic jurisprudence in the country, ISIS sent representatives to develop ties with them. ABM was estimated to have as many as two thousand fighters spread across its operational regions, but the majority of its combat power was in the Sinai Peninsula (ibid).

In order to strengthen ISIS position beyond Iraq and Syria, ISIS sent Musa'id Abu Qatmah as a representative to Sinai through the Gaza tunnel systems to convince the Egyptians to side with Al-Baghdadi.[54] The same month, men carrying three letters from a Libya based ISIS representative named Abu Ahmad al-Libi were dispatched to Sinai. Al-Libi encouraged the Sinai group to unite under ISIS in exchange for a massive influx of guns and funds (ibid). On November 11, 2014, ABM officially swore its loyalty oath to ISIS leader Al-Baghdadi in an audio recording released online and announced via Twitter (Al-Tamimi, 2016). Soon after it was released, Al-Baghdadi accepted their pledge.

3.4.5 Libya

In the ruins of post-Qaddafi Libya, the country quickly fell into chaos under the rule of militias throughout the country (Nance, 2016). ANSAs quickly emerged after the fall of Qaddafi in an effort to assert control over regional interests. In addition to trafficking (Shaw and Mangan, 2014) porous borders and a long history of jihadist networks, Libya's failed state was a perfect power vacuum for the rise of two (Nance, 2016) ANSAs in the area, AQ and ISIS.

At the instigation of post-Qaddafi's Libyan state, ISIS was of diminutive concern when compared to

---

54 See. al-Shahed.net. accessed; 1st October 2017. From. http://www.alshahed.net/index.php?option=com_content&view=article&id=112365:2014-09-03-18-46-36&catid=478:01-09-04-2014.

AQ. ANSAs like Libyan Islamic Fighting Group (LIFG)[55] was vigorous since the 1990s and were more often than not controlled by Qaddafi. After the demise of Qaddafi, AQ exploited the power vacuum by aligning itself with local ANSAs. Despite AQs activity and networking resources in the area, it wasn't long before delegations from a newly formed ISIS would begin to cultivate Libya as a part of its planned expansion (ibid). Fighters were flowing between Syria and Libya and the Islamic State to fight the Syrian Civil War (ibid).

Among these fighters were a group known as The Battar Brigade, who fought alongside ISIS fighters Dier Ez-Zor and in Mosul before returning home to Libya (Paul and Robertson, 2014). These fighters returned and began to work to unite various factions in Derna and encourage them to join the Islamic State (Nance, 2016). The return of these fighters coincided with the emergence of the Shura Council of Islamic Youth (MSSI) who was establishing Islamic jurisprudence. MSSI promised to eliminate infidels which included judges, local community leaders, politicians (ibid) etc. ISIS saw this as an opportunity for expansion so they sent leaders to discuss expansion in the region. On October 5, 2014, MSSI and other ANSAs declared bayat for ISIS. A mass gathering from various fractions arrived in Derna to swear allegiance to Al-Baghdadi (ibid). In an audio recording released November 13,

---

55 LIFG was linked to AQ.

2014, Baghdadi accepted the bayat plan (ibid). After having accepted the merger plan, Baghdadi announced that Libya would be divided into wiliyat. These would be al-Fazzan (south), Tarablus (west) and al-Barqa (east) (Hassan, 2015).

3.4.6 Tunisia

Not to mention that the Arab Spring began from Tunisia where small protests merged and started the Jasmine Revolution. Such protests engulfed West Asian states and North Africa. Tunisians are also the major contributor of foreign fighters in ISIS. Since 2011, relations between various ANSAs operating from Libya and Tunisia have only intensified. Some of these interactions date as far back as the 1980s (Nance, 2016). Many Tunisian jihadists trained in Libya with the support of the Qaddafi regime and returned to organise several attacks on Tunisian soil. Tunisia, after the revolution, became a haven for ANSAs like the Soufan Group. The towns such as Ben Gardane and Bizerte became prime ground for recruitment in ANSAs. ISIS uses these locations for smuggling crossroads (ibid). Kasserine with its proximity to the border with Algeria, makes a convenient location for remote meetings. The region is very mountainous making it a clandestine location for jihadi training and recruitment. The region is poverty prone making the youths vulnerable for recruitment into various ANSAs like ISIS and AQ.

After the Arab Spring, AQ support and sympathisers grew as one can see the expansion of AQIM engulfing many African countries so did ISIS hold. Tunisian ANSAs face a dilemma whether to join AQ or ISIS. Since ISIS propaganda has been louder than that of AQ, many fighters from this country have joined ISIS. This has led to more ISIS support from the local ANSAs. AQ also has a deep history rooted since its formation in 1988. Some groups still remain loyal to AQ while the others are more inclined towards ISIS. Such manifestation of various ANSAs aligning with ISIS and AQ has caused the violence to escalate threatening its tourism industry which is vital for the country's economy. It was in late 2014, ISIS announced its visibility in Tunisia, in a video calling for Tunisians to raise the flag of Islam and tear to shreds the flag of Gaulle and Napoleon (ibid).

ISIS announced that it intended to form a new province to be called the Wilayat Ifriqiya.[56] Soon after ISIS made an appearance to engulf Tunisia, three groups pledged bayat to ISIS; Uqba ibn Nafi Battalion,[57] Mujahidin of Tunisia al-Qayrawan-bayat,[58] and Jund al-Khilafah Tunisia (ibid).[59]

---

56 Throwback to the name of Tunisia in the medieval era.
57 Pledge of alliance, May 28, 2015 via Twitter.
58 Pledged via audio, May 18, 2015.
59 Pledged on March 31, 2015.

3.4.7 Algeria

Algerian ANSA only drew attention from 2014 when one of its groups pledged an alliance to ISIS. After a week, Herve Gourdel (French tourist guide) was killed. It was exposed in a video entitled *"A message with Blood to the French Government"* (Shankar, 2014). This atrocious act against a French citizen was believed to be done by ISIS sympathiser which was an answer to French airstrike against ISIS.[60] This was believed to be done by ANSA Jund al-Khilafa that broke from AQIM.

Jund al-Khilafa initially was AQ group that broke in September 2014, through communication by leader Abdelmalek Gouri. After breaking ties with AQ, Abdelmalek Gouri took an oath of allegiance to ISIS, claiming AQIM had deviated from the right path. He pledged his loyalty to ISIS leader. However, Abdelmalek Gouri was killed by the Algerian Army. Since then, Jund al-Khilafa was forced to go low making them hard to implement Islamic jurisprudence and capture the territories in the country (Nance, 2016).

3.4.8 Nigeria

In the Islamic Maghreb region, Nigeria consists of majority Muslim population making it the largest Muslim country in Africa. With such a massive Muslim

---

60 Countries brawling ISIS with an airstrike, ground forces et al will be discussed in next chapter.

majority in the country, there is no doubt that radical Islamic fundamentalism became a breeding ground in the country. Mohammed Yusuf founded ANSA and named it as Boko Harem (BH). Yusuf was inspired to create an ultraorthodox fundamentalist Islamic nation-state along the lines of the Taliban in Afghanistan. He accepted the salafi/jihadi school of thought called al-Wala wal Bara.[61] He believed, like the Taliban, that western practices in clothing, music art, science, immunisation, cultural diversity, and foods had corrupted the Muslim practice of sole devotion of the worship of God, to the exclusion of all else. He rejected that Earth was round, Darwinism and Evolution (ibid).

In the beginning, ISIS was not on the scene since the group was more inclined towards AQ model and followed their radical ideology of cleansing the society of infidels through perpetual jihad (ibid). Following the atrocities committed by BH, Yosuf was killed and Shekau took over. The new leader also followed Osama's doctrine spreading its sphere of influence in Chad and Niger with various attacks on civilians and policemen (ibid).

When ISIS began to gain momentum after the Arab Spring, BH felt that ISIS was truly following the doctrine of Islam and AQ was moving away from true principles. Not to mention ISIS had more magnetisation towards

---

61 It means; love of all things that are of God and detestation of all things un-Islamic.

their propaganda became of their way of manipulation and ideology. On March 7, 2015, Abu Bakr Shekau changed BHs alliance from AQ to ISIS (Jeremy, 2015). Shekau declared that all areas and territory under its control to be a part of ISIS and dedicated the caliphate. A month after the declaration of bayat/alliance BH renamed itself as *"Islamic State-West Africa Province"* (ISWAP). BH quickly took up the ISIS practices of releasing videos depicting mass executions of civilians and security forces (ibid).

3.4.9 Caucasus

During the 1995 war against the Russian Federation, thousands of foreign fighters from dozens of Islamic extremist groups fought to establish an Independent Islamic Republic of Chechnya. There was heavy involvement of educated, western vacation jihadists, principally from the U.K., along with a nascent propaganda effort through audio tapes, video, pamphlets and books produced in the West. The practice of videotaping the decapitation executions of Russian soldiers began during the war in Chechnya. The Russian forces finally enforced order on the breakaway republic with scorched-earth policies. Highly sophisticated Islamic-oriented Chechen militants departed in the region of Chechnya, Dagestan and Ingushetia, and travelled down to Iraq and Syria (Nance, 2016).

Tarkhan Tayumurazovich, also known as Omar the Chechen was a sergeant in the Gorgian Army who is now the Emir of Northern Syria. He commands a force nearing one thousand strong. There is also some link between AQ and Caucasian ANSAs. Islamic Caucasus Emirate (ICE) has been the primary jihad group in the area, but with the deaths of several top leaders, and the defections of several others, is losing ground to ISIS (ibid). As many as two thousand Russian citizens have joined the ISIS war in Syria (Joscelyn, 2015). Chechens also have a notable presence in the jihadi recruitment as motivated by Omar and this stimulated people following radical Islamic fundamentalism. Chechnya ANSAs have also grown in number making ISIS easy for radicalising the group to follow their ideology. On June 27, 2015, the Caucusus province issued its oath of allegiance to Al-Baghdadi, "Obeying the order of Allah, we are declaring our allegiance to Caliph Ibrahim ben Awwad ben Ibrahim al-Badri al-Qoureishi al-Husseini for obedience and subordination... We testify that all mujahedeen of the Caucasus are united in this decision, and there are no disagreements among us on this issue. (Mukhopadhyay, 2015)"

3.4.10 Khorasan

Following the Soviet invasion of 1979, Afghanistan became a breeding ground for ideological base of ANSAs following radical Islamic fundamentalist interpretation. Not to mention the contribution of various Islamic scholars from the region in epitomising radical Islamic fundamentalism in the region and beyond.[62] Khorasan region had been brewing base of various groups like AQ etc. making it one of the recruiting base for ISIS. In 2012, militants associated with ISIS started recruiting jihadists, primarily from the ANSAs like Lashkar-e-Jhangvi Said, in Pakistan (Kiran, 2014). In early 2014, ISIS began organising and funding local groups in Afghanistan to compete with the Taliban and AQ (Seth, 2015). By September 2014, two hundred militants (Nance, 2016) had left Pakistan to join ISIS. In October 2014, five regional Pakistani Taliban (ibid) commanders switched allegiances from Afghan Taliban leader to ISIS (ibid). Additional leaders pledged alliance in a January 10, 2015 video, including Saad Emirati of Logar Province, Ubaidah al-Peshwari of al-Tawhid in Peshawar, Sheikh Muhsin of Kunar province, Talha of Lakki Marwat, and Omar al-Malnsur of the Lal Masjid. The group calls itself the Islamic State of Khorasan, comprising Afghanistan, Pakistan and Parts of India (ibid).

In early January 2015, Shahidullah Shahid of Tehrik-i-Taliban Pakistan (TTP) declared an alliance with ISIS (Craig and Khan, 2015). Similarly, the other groups like Ansar-ul-Khilafat Wal-Jihad, Pakistani Jundullah, Lal Masjid and Jamia Hafsa declared direct support to ISIS (Nance, 2016). Groups like Jamat-ul-Ahrar,

---

62 Various scholars and their contribution in developing radical Islamic ideology is covered in the previous chapter.

Lashkar-e-Jhangvisaid and Ahl-e-Summat Wai Jamat declared indirect support to ISIS (ibid). Khorasan leadership has cultivated tentative ties to local Islamic militants through bribes, presumably from ISIS coffers. These groups have further extended their propaganda to Pakistani cities by distributing recruitment pamphlets and videos showing how other groups have pledged alliance to ISIS, this was done to engulf more supporters and groups to strengthen their foothold in Khorasan region.

3.4.11 Saudi Arabia

Saudi Arabia has a history of radical Islam, it was from this country that Wahhabism had emerged and the King of Saud had formally agreed on Wahhabism interpretation of Islam. A country with the history of Wahhabism in its roots did play a clandestine role in supporting ISIS at its initial days. It was not the country that supported ISIS but individual funding from various businesses was recorded. In Islam, a charity for a religious cause is considered one of the pillars of Islam; Zakat. On April 28, 2015, Saudi officials announced that between then and prior December, ninety-three people had been arrested on suspicion links to ISIS.[63] In the global recruitment of ISIS, Saudi has been one of the major suppliers of jihadist

---

63 See, in particular. "Saudi arrests 93 suspected of ISIS links," *Al-Arabia* Published April 28,2015; accessed Dec. 3, 2015: http://english.alarabia.net/en/News?middle-east/2015/04/28/Saudi-arrests-93-ISIS-linked-militants-.html

to Syria. This indicates how ISIS influence in Saudi Arabia has been manufactured with radical roots in itself. The fact that both Mecca and Medina lie in Saudi Arabia, and Baghdadi's belief that King of Saudi Arabia and his family are not legitimate custodians of Islam, are key reasons why ISIS, following in the footsteps of AQ, has targeted the leadership and the nation for destabilisation. King of Saudi Arabia has supported western power to curb radical activities in West Asia (Nawaf, 2014). In November 2014, Baghdadi delivered a speech exhorting ISIS supporters to turn on Saudi leaders (ibid):

> *"O sons of al-Haramayn (The two Holy Shrines of Mecca and Medina)…the serpent's head and the stronghold of the disease are there…draw your swords and divorce life, because there should be no security for the Saloul"*(ibid; 55).

Soon after this speech, on November 10, 2014, a group called Mujahideen of the Arabian Peninsula pledged allegiance to ISIS (Nance, 2016). It also appears that a number of unnamed, purportedly Saudi individuals have been posting images of written pledges of allegiance, including a cake in the shape of ISIS flag (ibid).

3.4.12 Yemen

Yemen is the most economically backward country in West Asia. The country has a history of the division just like Korea. From 1970 to 1990, North and South Yemen was an independent nation. It was in the late 1990s both were united. Soon after the reunion, the country has a history of civil war and power struggle. In 1994, a short civil war erupted. In 2012 President Saleh who had held power for thirty years was toppled in an election during the Arab Spring.[64] His Vice-President, Abdu Rabbu Mansour Hadi, was voted in, the only candidate in the ballot (Nance, 2016).

The Iranian-backed, Shi'ite Houthi tribes allied with Saleh and formed Houthi group which became another group competing with Al – Qaeda in Arabian Peninsula (AQAP). Houthi descended on Sana'a in September 2014, a move that culminated in an assault on the presidential palace in January 2015 and the subsequent ouster of Hadi, who left Yemen entirely on March 25, 2015 (Jeremy, 2015). The Houthis became an opponent of AQ when they started capturing provinces in Yemen which were earlier within AQs grip. When the war between the two ANSAs broke out, Saudi Arabia ordered for full-time military intervention under Operation Decisive Storm (Nance, 2015). Saudi involvement in Yemen's civil war helped ISIS gain traction.[65] The triangular war between

---

64 See, in particular. "Who are the Houthis in Yemen?" *New York Times.* Published Jan. 20, 2015; accessed Dec. 3, 2016: http://www.nytimes.com/2015/01/21/world/middleeast/who-are-the-houthis-of-yemen.html

65 For more on Saudi's involvement in Yemen, see. Williams Jennifer. 2015. "The Saudi Arabia Problem: Why a country at war with jihadists also fuels them," *Vox.* Accessed March 20, 2016: http://www.vox.com/2015/12/1/9821446/saudi-problem-isis

two ANSA and Saudi helped ISIS take the opportunity to penetrate into Yemeni territory. In early February, a band of fighters supporting AQAP transferred their loyalty to ISIS and another video appeared on April 24, 2015, where twelve masked men identifying themselves as Soldiers of the Caliphate in Yemen pledged alliance to the caliphate (Williams, 2015). The head of ISIS in Yemen is reportedly the Saudi Nasser al-Ghaydani, whose nom de guerre is Abu Bilal al-Harbi (Nance, 2016).

3.5 Financial Networks

How does ISIS pay a battle force of thousands of Islamic soldiers, and perhaps 100,000 (ibid) or more widows, pensioners, construction workers and government bureaucrats, and still manages to buy cases of Red Bull, Vehicles for inspection and transportation, ammunition 7.62 x 39mm (ibid) for its foreign fighters? The leadership of ISIS has the firm conviction that ISIS can supply all of its citizens with modern trappings of a sovereign entity. Public benefit programmes such as universal healthcare, manufacturing women's clothing, mandatory primary schooling and arming and equipping an Islamic army requires an extraordinary amount of money (ibid).

In order to understand the initial financial network of ISIS one need to look back at the Arab Spring. When Arab Spring took off Basher Assad used force to suppress Sunni uprisings that were anti-Assad and his regime, they wanted to throw Assad out of power but his military capability could not be crushed. NATO countries also wanted to throw Basher Assad out of power but Article 2 (4) of the UN Charter (Shaw, 2008) stopped them from militarily intervene in Syria. The U.S, U.K. and other NATO members along with few Gulf countries (Saudi Arabia, Qatar and Kuwait) started funding Sunni rebels to throw Assad out of power but the funding went into the hands of jihadi fighters who were mostly comprised of Sunni rebels under the command of Baghdadi under ISI at that time. With this the initial funding of the organisation began and when ISI transpired into ISIS the organisation was better off with their own taxation and revenue, they had also captured a major portion of Iraq and Syria and oil fields fell under the control of ISIS commandeering 10–15 oil fields (Hosken, 2015) in the region. The enumeration of ISIS fighters are around $400 (Stern and Berger, 2015) and for child soldiers they pay $100 (ibid) now the question revolves where do they get so much money from?

ISIS is considered the world's best-financed ANSA due to the cash and natural resources they looted from the populations and regions they seized in Iraq and Syria. And they use a myriad of methodologies to raise money for their proto-state. Some funds came from the direct theft of gold and cash from the banks of Raqqa, Mosul, Fallujah, and Ramadi; more comes from stolen oil produced on stolen oil fields and distilled in stolen refineries, then sold on the black market in the bordering states (Nance, 2016). But this is just the tip of the financial iceberg.

3.5.1 Theft

ISIS has a wide and more diversified theft portfolio that includes the licence and sale of antiquities, the seizure of cars and jewellery (Giovanni, Mcgrath et al, 2014), human trafficking of captured women as wives or sex-slaves and ransom from the kidnapping of the men (Hosken, 2015). ISIS has made millions from kidnappings and it is reported that the group has made $20 million by kidnappings a year 2014 (Stanley, 2015). Leaving kidnappings they have also looted banks of whichever city fell under its control. When ISIS ran over Iraq's second largest city they looted $429 million (ibid). ISIS has also set up ministries of antiquities where it sells historical artefacts in the black market, when they ran over the remains of Palmyra they destroyed the historical remains and precious historical statues were sold off in the black market. Altogether they earned $100 million (ibid) a year trading in antiquities. The most significant liquid possessions that were stolen by ISIS, in this case cash were robbed from a series of banks in Iraq. ISIS's bank theft together dwarfs the scale of the $70 million (Cam and Philips, 2015) theft at the Banco Central in Brazil in 2005, the largest heist in the world to that point. The total sum of stolen in this series of bank thefts by ISIS is estimated to have been somewhere between $500 million to $1 billion (ibid).

ISIS has also seized an immense amount of land, along with the agricultural assets fount on it: entire silos of wheat and barley, tons of baled cotton and wool, and grazing animals. Many of these agricultural commodities were then sold within Syria or smuggled across the borders, adding an immense sum to the coffers of the caliphate. For instance, ISIS acquired as much as $200 million (Nance, 2015) in potential value from its newly confiscated wheat silos in Iraq alone. All told, ISIS now has land in its possession in Tigris and Euphrates river region that in the past has generated around half of the wheat yield in Syria, about a third of the wheat in Iraq, and nearly 40 (Cam and Philips, 2015) percent of the barley in Iraq. Even if the annual grain yield of this ISIS farmland were sold illicitly outside of the caliphate, it still might generate as much as $200 million (ibid) in income a year.

3.5.2 Donations

Donations to ISIS from charity/zakat by rich sympathisers have arrived in a valise filled with cash by private plane or handed over at the border of the caliphate. Many of these come from wealthy donors, or from donation bundlers based in Qatar, Kuwait, Saudi Arabia or Dubai. According to the *Washington Post* it was reported that ISIS received $40 million (Stanley, 2015) in 2013–2014 from rich businessmen and family from Saudi Arabia, Kuwait, Qatar and UAE. Kuwait arrested six men for funding ISIS and Saudi Arabia arrested 500 men (ibid) for linkages with ISIS and funding and some were even trying to start oil marketing with ISIS in Black Market. This led to the flow of money from these Gulf countries to ISIS (ibid).

3.5.3 Oil

One of the single largest income sources of ISIS is Oil. When ISIS seized a large swath of Iraq in 2014, they came to control numerous small Iraqi oilfields including the Ajil, Hamrin, Jawan, Taza, Najma, Qasab, West Tikrit and Qayarah (Dhiman, 2015). In addition to the oil under the ground they acquired oil wells, small refineries, oil pipelines, and oil storage depots. The Iraq Energy Institute estimates that ISIS had around 350 (Giovanni, Mcgrath et al, 2014) oil wells in Iraq alone, 45 (ibid) of which it then lost as a result of US airstrikes and recapture by Kurdish pershmerga. As it retreated, ISIS set fire to some of the wells that it lost (ibid).

According to an International Energy Agency report published in October 2014, when ISIS first seized its oil assets, it acquired a fair amount of initial oil supplies. Since 2014, ISIS has controlled around 60 percent (Nance, 2016) of Syria's ability to produce oil production capacity and 80 percent (ibid) of Syria's stored pre-war oil. It began by draining around 3 million (ibid) barrels of oil from four oil pipelines as well as from a series of storage depots pumping stations (ibid).

The oil assets ISIS stole are now being used to create a supply of fuel for its own cars, trucks, tanks, and armed personnel carriers; to generate electricity for ISIS territories; and to provide fuel to the 8–10 million (ibid) Iraqis and Syrians under their control. This stolen oil also furnishes ISIS with a source of revenue from the sales to a variety of parties: the Assad regime, the Kurds, other Syrian ANSAs, international aid agencies, Turkey and other nations that currently share a border with ill-defined and shifting landscape of the Islamic State (ibid). US intelligence agencies estimate that ISIS collected black market oil revenue of approximately $100 million (Smith, Arkhipov, Meyer et al, 2015) in 2014 after seizing major parts of Iraq and acquiring oilfields and pipelines in both Iraq and Syria. After a year of almost unmolested operations, the US Treasury Department intelligence estimates these ISIS-controlled oil fields have generated around $500 million (ibid) in 2015. This estimate is convincing as a document taken from ISIS's Ministry of Finance reveals that they took in approximately $46.7 million (Hendawi, Hamza et al, 2015) in April 2015, which gave an annual average of approximately $560 million (ibid). According to Peter Galbraith, an adviser to Kurdish government in the matters of oil, believes that the amount generated by ISIS could possibly be higher than $800 million (ibid) per annum because of ISIS selling of oil in oil scarce countries like Syria, Turkey and others. They are selling oil in black for $200 (ibid) a barrel.

Initially, ISIS moved oil through giant oil tanker trucks in order to transport its fuel in a larger area surrounding bordering countries in Syria and Iraq. This was done because they did not have an oil pipeline from where they could transfer oil in the black market. However, these tankers became vulnerable to air strikes so ISIS started using smaller oil trucks for supply in the black market across the countries. In countries like Syria and Turkey, oil scarcity is there so brokers and middlemen were used to trading these oils to reduce suspicion. Mostly ISIS used tunnels to deliver fuels to other countries and groups. At first when they were using bigger tankers, air strikes destroyed all their resources. In order to avoid such attacks ISIS used small tankers and it worked for them because these small trucks were not suspected of delivering oil to the black market (nance, 2016).

3.5.4 Taxation

After establishing a caliphate, ISIS has gone just beyond any ordinary ANSA to an Islamist state. According to Daniel Glaser, Assistant Secretary of the Treasury for Terrorist Financing says that ISIS is bringing in hundreds of millions a year in taxes on commerce alone (Hendawi, Hamza et al, 2015). In the ISIS capital of Raqqa for instance, ISIS taxes all goods that are being imported, exported, or transported. This includes a tax on items being smuggled, such as looted antiquities, an illicit activity that is in violation of the tenets of Islam (Giovanni, Mcgrath et al, 2014).

ISIS is known to have a variety active taxing methods, fee, or shakedown scheme. For instance, some citizen-subjects of ISIS have to pay 10 percent (ibid) tax on their bank withdrawal (besides having their banks robbed from time to time by ISIS), while police, soldiers, and teachers are allowed to repent for having served under a secular Ba'athist regime by getting their own atonement ID for a mere $2,500 (Cam and Philips, 2015) with an added annual fee of $200 (ibid) a year for good measure. ISIS is also gaining revenue from income taxes, a 10 percent (Giovanni, Mcgrath et al, 2014) zakat charity fee on small business, taxes on crops and farms animals, taxes on those who provide humanitarian aid (ibid), rent on former regime's buildings, profits skimmed from the business it now runs, textbook fees, road tolls and driving fines, cleaning fees for stall merchants, taxes on water and electrical bills, as well as fines for inappropriate clothing or lighting up a cigarette or pipe (Nance, 2016). Control over water has also enabled ISIS to continue to fight the regimes in West Asia. It has seized dams next to conquered areas and also has a flooded area to have a military advantage during warfare. Tabqa Dam and Assad on Euphrates River in Syria have helped ISIS to generate electricity to Aleppo which it controls. ISIS has collected taxes from the electricity which it provides to the cities in Syria and Iraq.

3.6 Weaponries

The weapon that ISIS uses against other ANSAs and countries were all confiscated from Syria, Iraq and Libya or exported to the region through middlemen across borders of Turkey. Huffington Post reported that the most common sources of weapons used by ISIS militants were manufactured in the US and captured in Iraq, and Russian-made goods captured from the Syrian army (Nance, 2016). Conflict Armament Research suggests that many arms given to the moderate Syrian rebels by the allied nations are now in possession of ISIS, who overran the rebels. Much of the ammunition was manufactured in Russia but distributed to allied nations by the US. Nevertheless, weapons from Austria, Poland, Belgium, Romania, China, Russia, Croatia, South Africa, France, Soviet Union, Germany, UAE, Iran, US, Italy and former Yugoslavia are also in ISIS arsenal (ibid).

The weapon utilised by ISIS were overwhelmingly captured from the Iraqi military and police headquarters and checkpoints, the Assad regime military, the Free Syrian Army, or from other major players fighting the Syrian conflict. ISIS has also acquired weapons from the black market, but it's simpler to get them from arsenals and depots (ibid). ISIS also acquired or captured weapons from other ANSAs. According to Bellingcat Investigation Project, ISIS had access to a variety of weapons such as rocket launchers, grenade launchers, and American made M60 machine guns (Christopher, 2014) from

Saudi Arabia. According to Bellingcat founder Eliot Higgins, weapons were first sold to Saudi Arabia and then flown to Turkey, then smuggled into Syria, where they were either given or sold to ISIS by sympathisers (ibid).

The number of weapons in the hands of ISIS is hard to estimate and not easy to come by. During the capture of Mosul in 2014, ISIS took 2,300 Humvees (Nance, 2016), over 100 wheeled vehicles (ibid), and tons of tracked vehicles. Most of the vehicles were acquired from Camp Speicher near Tikrit (ibid).

3.6.1 Vehicles

The Land Cruiser 70 (ibid) and the Hilux (ibid) are a series of compact pickup trucks marketed by the Japanese manufacturer Toyota. The Toyota pickup has a reputation for toughness and does particularly well in the tough terrain of Syria, Iraq, Libya, Yemen and Afghanistan. It also makes regular appearances in ISIS propaganda videos (ibid). Other countries have often asked Japanese company Toyota about ISIS using its vehicles for raid and propaganda but the company doesn't know about how it passed on to ISIS. Military spokesperson of Iraq believes that these vehicles have been smuggled into the country by middlemen (Engel, 2015). During 2014–2015, an Australian newspaper reported that 800 Toyota (ibid) trucks were missing from regular inventories and might have been exported to Iraq (ibid). Toyota trucks and other vehicles were given to FSA and other ANSAs during the Syrian Civil War. When ISIS swept through different regions in Syria and Iraq including police and army headquarters, these vehicles were captured by ISIS. ISIS uses Toyota to convey militants and as technical vehicles by screwing a variety of heavy weapons on the rear of the truck bed and adding the seal of the caliphate. The number of Toyotas used by ISIS is unknown but it could be next to hundreds or thousands (Nance, 2016).

Ford company had also exported a large amount of their vehicle to the security forces of Iraq. Many of these vehicles were fully armoured. Hundreds fell into ISISs grip as they captured major cities like Mosul and others (Hosken, 2015).

ISIS has also been known to use US and allied nations manufactured vehicles. US vehicles include the M1114 armoured Humvees (Nance, 2016), wheeled and tracked vehicles and five to six-ton trucks (ibid). In 2008, the US and Iraq signed three contracts for the sale of vehicles and other equipment. On April 22, 2009, the US exported 5000 Humvees (ibid) and by July 2009, the Iraqi forces had 8,000 Humvees (ibid). When the US troops withdrew from Iraq, they sold 3,500 Humvees (ibid) to Iraq, out of which 3,000 Humvees (ibid) were heavily armoured. When ISIS started capturing territories in Syria and Iraq, they captured US manufactured vehicles from Iraq and Russian vehicles from Syria. ISIS captured a number of Armoured Fighting Vehicles (AFV) (ibid) at that time. 50 (ibid) Russian-made MT-LB Armoured Personnel

Carries (ibid), 47 US made M1117 ASV (ibid), 7 Russian-made BMP-1 (ibid), 82 US made M1113 (ibid) and four Ukrainian made BTR-80 (ibid) were captured by ISIS.

3.6.2 Improvised Explosive Devices(IEDs)

All of these captured vehicles were not used to transfer fighters and ammunition etc. Many of such vehicles captured by ISIS were transformed into Suicide Vehicle-Borne Improvised Explosive Devices (SVBIEDs). In Syria and Iraq, ISIS captured roughly more than 100 vehicles that were further transformed into SVBIEDs. SVBIEDs of ISIS are varied in type, but they have been using primarily US made equipment because the US vehicles are not simple for mechanics so they transformed these vehicles. When attacking well-defended bases, ISIS relied heavily on breaching gates and perimeters using SVBIEDs (ibid). These types of vehicles that ISIS has transformed include: SVBIED – Sedan, SBVIED-Bongo, SBVIED-Minivan, SVBIED Dumptruck/Cement Mixer/Water Tanker, SV-BMP, SV-M 113 Bombvee, SVB-LTVR and Bomb-Cat, Bomb-RAP (ibid).

ISIS has also been using human bombs to attack their enemies. These weapons are used as vests or belts in order to use them in human form so that killing would be easier. These weapons used in humans for attacks are known as Suicide Pedestrian-Borne Improvised Explosive Device. SPBIEDs are frequently used by

ISIS in West Asia and beyond. There are three types of SPBIED that are used by ISIS. Offensive Combat SPBIED; used in men when the enemy approaches they blow up. Western countries recognise them as jihadi suicide bombers (ibid).

3.6.3 Tanks and Artillery

ISIS has mostly targeted Russian-made tanks because it seems comfortable to use with easy reparation and less complicated. When ISIS had captured US tanks, they could not fully operate these US made tanks so they stripped machines guns and ammunition off these tanks and blew them up (Nance, 2016). Most of the tanks ISIS possessed from Iraqi and Syrian forces.

ISIS captured Towed Artillery and Multiple Rocket Launchers from Iraq and Syria. They captured 2 Russian 2A18 (D-30) Howitzer, six Russian D-74 Field Gun, 52 US M198 Howitzer and two Chinese Type 63 Rocket Launcher (ibid). In ISIS propaganda video *Clanging of the Sword 1–4, Defiant of the Sword* (Stern and Berger, 2015) and other propaganda videos posted in YouTube, Anti-Tank and Anti-Aircraft weaponry system were also seen (Hosken, 2015). They captured 3 Russian 9M17 Scorpion Anti-Tank (Nance, 2016), 1 Russian M113 Konkurs Anti-Tank (ibid), 2 Russian 9M133 Anti-Tank (ibid), 90 Russian KPV Anti-Aircraft (ibid), 7 Russian ZPU-1 Anti-Aircraft (ibid), 1 Russian ZPU-2 Anti-Aircraft (ibid), 31 Russian ZU-23 Anti-Aircraft (ibid) and two Chinese Type 65 Anti-Defence (ibid). The irresistible preponderance of Anti-Aircrafts are accumulated on Toyota vehicles and technologies are used as an anti-position weapon.

The acquisition of Manual Portable Air-Defence System by Assad regime went into the hands of other ANSAs including ISIS. It is estimated that the Assad regime had stockpiled 20,000 (Brent, 2014) MANPADS which were later captured by FSA. It is rumoured that ISIS acquired between 250–400 anti-aircraft (ibid) missiles systems such as the Russian SA-18 and SA-24 Grinch MANPADS (ibid) when it seized Tabqa airbase in Syria. ISIS has conducted a limited number of MANPADS attacks against the Syrian air force or US coalition air forces. ISIS-Sinai in Egypt has shot down two aircraft with SA-16 IGLAs (Nance, 2016); one was a Mi-17, killing five soldiers (ibid) and an AH-64 Apache helicopter gunship (ibid). These may have come from Libyan stocks (ibid). According to a report by Iraqi news, ISIS militants targeted US A-10 Thunderbolt aircraft using 9K32 Strela-2 MANPADS (Brent, 2014) when the planes carried out air strikes on ISIS positions near Mosul, Iraq (ibid).

3.6.4 Small Arms and Light Infantry Weapons

Conflict Armament Research concluded that ISIS was mostly using Russian, US and Chinese weapons to fight its enemies. Not to mention ISIS overrun of a territory helped them acquire many weapons that were supplied by various countries. When ISIS fought Iraqi forces, Iraqi forces retreated and left 30,000 Kalashnikovs (Nance, 2016). In battle and raid, ISIS also captured weapons from Syrian troops. ISIS now has 30,000 (ibid) and more Russian, Chinese, Romanian, Hungarian, East Germany, Bulgarian, Polish, Iraqis and former Yugoslavian manufactured AK-47, 7400 (ibid), US manufactured M16, 2 Belgium made FN FAL and two Chinese CQ (ibid).

ISIS militants are also seen using Croatian Elmech EM-992 sniper rifle (ibid), Chinese PKM M80 machine guns (ibid) and Chinese type 79 sniper rifle (ibid). There is no evidence showing how ISIS acquired these sniper rifles. Other than these weapons, ISIS is seen using drones with the camera for surveillance. In August 2014, ISIS released a video showing its forces using a drone at the Syrian Army Brigade 93 Base (ibid). Iraqi security analyst Alex Mello noted that ISIS also used drones in Zawbaa and Fallujah to coordinate fighting in those regions. In October 2015, Iraqi security forces announced that they had downed a drone belonging to ISIS east of Ramadi. That was a fixed-wing drone similar to the RQ-9. Other reports cite the use of the Phantom FC-40, Phantom QR-X350 programmable drones, and eyewitness have spotted Skywalker X& and Skywalker X8 drones in Iraq (ibid).

3.7 State Under ISIS

Prophet Muhammad's (PBHU) version of an Islamic State is described in his document called *Constitution of Medina*.

PBHU was exiled from his city and home Mecca by Quarysh tribe, which was his own tribe. The Prophet was thus given refuge by the people of Medina which is a town little more than two hundred miles directly north, up the Hijaz Peninsula of what is now Saudi Arabia. In 622 CE, the people of Medina asked PBHU to write the constitution. The result was a social-military contract for the city's population, a third of who were Jews. The constitution was drawn up to recognise the rights of the city's minorities, namely the Jews, as well as to deal with the military threat posed by the bellicose Quaraysh from Mecca. The document consisted of sixty-three articles (ibid), of which ten specifically related to the religious rights of the nine main Jewish tribes of Medina (ibid). Article 30 (ibid), for example stated that the Jews of Banu Awf to be considered community among Muslim. They were to be guaranteed right to freedom among Muslims (ibid). The Jews were required to pay a proportionate liability of war expenses along with the believers in the on-going struggle against the Quraysh, so long as they continue to fight in conjunction with them (ibid).

As the time passed by, various alterations were made and later after the split between the variants more reformation followed.[66] Countries started following Islamic jurisprudence as seen in countries like Iran after 1979, Saudi Arabia etc. they way of controlling the state solely depends on the Islamic jurisprudence.

---

66   Islamic Fundamentalism is covered in the previous chapter

As with an increase of ANSAs epitomised by radical Islamic interpretation, various reformations were seen that fuelled such ANSAs moving away from a theocratic model. Similarly, in the case of ANSAs like AQ, the reformation and jurisprudence depended solely on Bin Laden's interpretation of Islam. Same is the case with ISIS. Baghdadi as an Islamic scholar would know a great deal about the Constitution of Medina: his Islam-based cult purports to recreate the earliest days of the Prophets and the two golden generations that followed him. So it seems curious that the Constitution of Medina more than 1,300 years old (ibid) should be so at odds of ISIS.

When it comes to controlling the captured territory, ISIS's ideological fantasy is seen overlapping with the control mechanism. In a very real sense, ISIS runs the world's largest prison, with all aspects of life enthralled by a cult interpretation of the earliest days of Sharia law. Their belief system brings twenty-first century Muslims to live precisely to live as Muslims in the seventh century world, but with electricity and automatic weapons; a system designed to focus every aspect of the inhabitants lives about what constitutes a proper diet, or how they should dress on the street in order to live solely for God, even when in violation of all previous fourteen centuries of Islamic law and tradition. ISIS controls all aspect of life, from price controls in the market to the elimination of music, art, and culture not related to religious observances. They hold control with dictatorial grip, and allow only their own soldiers to administer justice, mediate civil disagreements, and determine what one can and cannot do in their self-proclaimed caliphate (ibid).

ISIS uses Hisbah[67] who acts as an internal security police force. Hisbah controls every aspect of life in ISIS-held territories. Their mission is to ensure that the people under ISIS control now live according to the observances of seventh century tribes of the Western Arabia desert. The Hisbah accomplishes this with soft-spoken intimidation, arrests, trial and punishment, including death (ibid). In ISIS propaganda videos, Hisbah is seen patrolling the streets of ISIS territories to make sure that Sharia has been followed by the people in a proper manner. Any vice that is not sanctioned such as alcohol, smoking, drug use, playing music, western games, wearing un-Islamic clothing, theft, non-sanctioned personal violence, slandering, blaspheming, having illicit sex, or adultery falls under their purview. The Hisbah also enforces religious ruling, price controls, mediate small disputes among people et al. On a practical level, this manifests as a liberty to meddle openly in the details of day to day lives of passer-by, and since the Hisbah is mainly a foreign contingent, they routinely undermine the sense of self-esteem and autonomy of Syrians and Iraqis.[68]

---

67 Hisbah is an Arabic terminology which means accountability. For ISIS, Hisbah means being accountable to God's doctrine.
68 See, in particular. "The Islamic State (Part 4)," *Vice*.2014. Accessed Dec. 12.2016: http://news.vice.com/video/the-islamic-state-part-4

Hisbah is properly organised into battalions under the Sharia law emir and operate in two-man or one men vehicle of squads police. They are covered with a white dress or Dishdashas and carry AK-47 and other weapons to make sure that people are under control and obey by strict Sharia law (ibid).

People who violate Islamic Sharia law are given death sentence and are killed in public with stones. ISIS has implemented strict Islamic law re-establishing Islamic jurisprudence and they patrol the captured cities and villages to assure that no violations are being made. There were executions in the region and first were the priest who refused to pledge an alliance to ISIS, doctors were killed who refused to treat IS soldiers and there were killing of those who betrayed the Islamic State and collaborated with the governments in Iraq and Syria (Hosken, 2015). Men were ordered to attain prayers five times a day punctually. Schools are segregated with gender and western ideology books were burnt down and were not allowed in the region because they wanted to educate the youth with fundamentalist values. The aim of this violence is to bring in public order in the region and it is divided into three; first for those who opposed ISIS, aim is to threaten them with cruelty and violence; second for those who are already followers of ISIS the idea was to bring them under proper grab of the regime; third for those who are undecided are to be influenced under ISIS ideology, threaten them and understand if they would condone the violence and remain silent (Stern and Berger, 2015).

In ISIS society, women are subordinate to a level of oppression and brutality that was last seen in the eighth century; they are essentially slaves. Many compare ISIS's control of women to Saudi Arabia or Afghan culture, but the role of women in Raqqa and occupied cities make those societies seem relatively liberal. Women are regarded as virtual non-entities, apart from acting as nursemaids to the children of jihadist fighters, and preparing the boys to become child soldiers and the girls to become marriage chattel. The women are expected to constantly keep their education limited to waging jihad and maintaining only ISIS's version of Islamic cultism (Nance, 2016). As one woman said *"Jihad brings the promise of a heavenly reward… Women are primarily tasked to assist their men in their jihadist duty"* (Alami, 2014).

ISIS does have a force to control women activities and check that they sand by the Islamic jurisprudence/Sharia law. The *al-Khansaa*brigades and *Umm Rayhan* brigades are paramilitary forces supporting Hisbah religious police force. Each of these brigades operates in their own women stations as these brigades consist of women police forces. In order to join these two forces, women must be of 18–25 (Nance, 2016) and must be a virgin. They get paid $75 per month (ibid)[69] and are authorised to carry AK-47 rifles (ibid). The brigades have two types of units: Morality police and a counterintelligence combat support unit. European volunteers join the combat support arm at checkpoints and search the bodies of women to detect female disguised male infiltrators. However, Arab women patrol the streets and enforce the oppressive laws against their own (ibid). A significant role for the two brigades of women is to strike women wearing make-up, high heels, prescribed clothes et al. These people are stroked with a cane. More harsh punishment is given to women who try to evade or escape and sometimes they are even beaten to death.

The term "Sex Jihad" has become an eminent terminology on the internet. These are young women who travel all the way to Syria and Iraq in the name of Hijrah and promise a child to ISIS fighter as their contribution to jihad. The prospective jihadi bride's award is to be allowed to marry a cult-sanctioned soon to be a martyr.[70] In ISIS's caliphate, the dress code for women is a serious concern for them. They ask women

---

69　Now that ISIS is losing ground, their salaries must have been reduced. Even for fighters it is believed that salaries have been reduced.

70　See. Agence France-Presse. 2013. "Sex Jihad Raging in Syria, Claims Minister," *Telegraph*. Accessed August, 12, 2015: http://www.telegraph.co.uk/news/worldnews/middleeast/syria/10322578/Sex-Jihad-raging-in-Syria-claims-minister.html.

to cover themselves over their entire body so that no skin and no female form may be apparent, or the women may be arrested or beaten by the religious police, al-Hisabah, or their all-female al-Khansaa and Umm Rayhan enforcer brigades (Mahmood, 2015). They make women wear Abaya, Hijab and Nijab.

ISIS has used the methodology of brainwashing children in the caliphate. They used their own interpretation of Islam to radicalise children and once they are radicalised, they are trained to be a part of their Global Jihad. Recruiting child soldiers is their unique strategy of warfare. However, the usage of children as war machines was seen during Pol Pot's Khmer Rouge. Children are brainwashed for adopting the ideology of radical Islam. ISIS schools are strictly gender-segregated; in fact, the education of girls is not a priority in occupied regions as much as the control of their morals and bodies (Bloom, 2015). Children are trained in various camps and used as soldiers. In ISIS's videos there were visuals of children beheading Iraqi and Syrian soldiers. First they are trained with teddy bears and later when they master the art of ISIS then they are used as soldiers and executioners (Nance, 2016).

Approximately eight million people (ibid) live under the self-styled ISIS, in order to control the massive population, healthcare is necessary with other facilities as well for survival. ISIS has converted captured buildings of government offices into hospitals, prisons etc. the most important of it is healthcare where delivery of healthcare in ISIS is characterised by a very low doctor-patient ratio of 1:500,000 (ibid). Most doctors and healthcare professionals have left or have gone underground. Reason for this is modern medical practice is secular and often incompatible with theoretical directives. Practitioners of the modern secular style in ISIS can be subjected to intimidation, abuse and even death. This has made doctors escape from ISIS healthcare. Only a few dozen healthcare professionals have immigrated to join ISIS but they are medically insignificant although they represent a powerful propaganda tool for ISIS. Most of their healthcare centre was destroyed during air strike done by Russia, US and other countries (ibid).

The form of *Hudud*[71] could be best described as "*Hudud Ultra*." They have arranged for all punishments to be carried out in the precise manner of seventh century Islam. In fact ISIS has codified an excessive form of Hudud in order to eliminate any tolerance or compromise that was adopted since the Qur'an was written. That makes the ISIS variation for more inflexible than even the most of stifling extremes of the Qur'anic and Hadith based Hudud found in Saudi Arabia (Heather, 2016). Each ISIS organisation has a Sharia law advisory

---

71 Hudud is a word used in Islamic law to describe the acceptable practice of issuing punishments for crimes that violate the social order. The word Hudud is plural of the Arabic word had, which means limitations or restriction.

committee and a judiciary. The Sharia court for each level from the highest command to the street level brings the transgressor before them, listens to the case, and doles out the punishment. Usually the prisoners are held for some time in a Hisbah jail, as there is often a long waiting list for punishments (Nance, 2016). It depends on the crimes committed whether a prisoner is beaten or killed. The execution methodologies carried out by ISIS include gun execution, beheading one or more victims, decapitation through explosives detonation cord, death by dragging, death by drowning, immolation, explosive execution, death by burial, death by mashing, stoning to death, death by falling and crucifixion (ibid). The method varies with crimes committed in the caliphate. Each crime has a different method of killing in the ISIS state.

3.8 Conclusion

It is lucid that ISIS has emerged as one of the affluent ANSAs epitomised by radical Islamic interpretation. Following post 9/11 period, ISIS has emerged as a new type of transnational threat. It has been able to maintain its autonomy, outstretch, structure etc. despite the constantly changing international security environment. In terms of modus operandi, ISIS has been able to distance itself from the state and the state system in general by moving into transnational space and effectively using their ideology, recruitment system, financial mechanisms etc.

Despite regional bipolar rivalry in West Asia and internal tension in Iraq and Syria, ISIS has emerged as a significant player in IR. They have exploited state vulnerabilities and have expanded beyond West Asia through alliances and attacks. ISIS access to sophisticated weapons, oil, trade routes etc. where the government is weak and international system hesitant, allowed ISIS to thrive and expand. ISIS's financial mechanisms, hierarchical system, affiliates etc. is a symbol of evolution within ANSAs. ISIS has used a great degree of management and manipulation where various other groups have formed an alliance with ISIS and they have also succeeded in magnetising more fighters in the group dwarfing other ANSAs like Al-Qaeda etc. It is apparent from the above discussions that ISIS has emerged as a formidable ANSA in the post 9/11 period.

ISIS and Its Implications for International Relations

4.1 Introduction

Over the past decades, the world has been engulfed by religion in a massive way. Starting with Israel's victory in the June 1967 Six-Day War, which initiated a link between Zionism and Religious Orthodox in Israel, and continuing through the 9/11 attacks to the rise of ISIS. Religion has therefore been a driving factor in relations among and within states. Scholars like Timothy Shah (2012) pointed that religion has now emerged as one of the most significant and influential factors in global affairs but remains the least examined factors in the professional study and practice of world affairs.

Religion is under-theorised in IR because of the dominant notions such as secularism, democracy, nation-state etc. all of which are the product of western-centric knowledge system. This chapter will provide analysis on waves of theorising religion and IR by looking at contemporary developments to the rise of ISIS where religion has become a cause for augmented international conflicts.

4.2 Religion and International Relations

History has been characterised by a thorough interpretation of religion and another aspect of society so that today's global resurgence of religion is actually better characterised as a return to business as usual. The combination of a grudging intellectual realisation that social science needs to deal with religion, in combination with dramatic examples of religion reasserting itself into international politics, is starting to put religion on the intellectual and policy agendas (Bellin, 2008).

There are literature and theoretical signposts those points towards a deeper understanding of how religion has been playing a significant role in global politics. Much of it has remained under-theorised in the vast universe of IR. The result, as Monica Duffy Toft observes is that traditional international relations theory provides little guidance for those needing to understand the interplay of religion and politics in a global setting (Duffy, 2012).

Mainstream IR paradigms have focused more on secularisation thesis thus overlooking the role of religion in IR. There are three elements of mainstream secularisation thesis: First, it maintains that there is an increasing distinction between religious and secular realm.

Second, religious belief becomes most appropriately consigned to the private sphere and also under the department of states itself. Finally, this privatisation of religion is the sine qua non of liberal democracy. Such secularisation thesis heavily shaped the political thought of western societies, but in particular it thrives in IR. The reason for this rejection of religion as a separate entity for theoretical analysis remains because such secularisation thesis literally had its origins in the rejection of religion itself by the Treaty of Westphalia.

Because of this foundational background, mainstream IR paradigms hardly mention religion. As Eva Bellin examines that the tendency to ignore religion can be traced to the theological inspiration drawn from the works of Marx, Durkheim and Weber. All three theorists believed that religion was a pre-modern relic, destined to fade with the advantage of industrialisation, urbanisation, bureaucratisation and rationalisation (Bellin, 2001).

Religion has been one of the major sources of international conflicts for many centuries. The rise of political Islam has powerfully reinforced secularism in the West, more than any other single religious or political tradition. Islam has come to represent the non-secular in European and American political thought and practices. Secularism has been consolidated in part through opposition to the idea of an anti-modern, anti-Christian and theocratic Islamic Middle East (Hurd, 2008).

There is another body of opinion that holds that is precisely the process of modernisation that is producing the current religious resurgence. Samuel P. Huntington explained that the process of economic modernisation and social change throughout the world are separating people from long-standing local identities. They also weaken the nation-state as a source for identity. In much of the world, religion has moved in to fill this gap, often in the forms of movements that are labelled fundamentalists (Huntington, 1993).

There is a wide array of view that opposes religion as the main cause for international conflicts. This is done by the sympathisers of the secularisation thesis. If the secularisation thesis is correct on religion and war then one should observe three developments from their thesis. First, the number of religious believers should decrease. Second, out of the wars that are fought, they should not have different religious reasons for the wars that are fought. Finally, the brawny substantiation for secularisation thesis would be the decline of religious wars that are fought (Mueller, 1989).

It is problematic to challenge the developments observed from secularisation thesis because wars are among the most complex of social phenomena, and disentangling other elements of war from religious would be a significant historical and contemporary challenge. Given that religion has no role to play in international conflicts, there is a wave of scholarly contribution on religion and international relations that have taken theoretical analysis in IR to another level. IR paradigms are mainly confined to traditionalist, positivist and post-positivist. And the debate of theoretical implication on world politics also remains confined to these three. However, building a theoretical analysis on religion and international relations should not be confined to these three debates nor should it be looked to challenge the existing paradigms in IR. Religion and international relations should be looked as beyond post-positivist paradigm that would show ways to scholars attempting to understand international relation from the prism of religion.

In the mainstream IR paradigm, sovereign states competing with one other is taken into analytical account but NSA/ANSAs does not fit in mainstream IR paradigms. Theory of Open Source Anarchy opened an analysis on NSA/ANSAs. According to OSA theory, an international system which was a closed system where only sovereign states were considered as prominent actors have now become open where NSA/ANSAs have penetrated the global politics as significant actors. Now when these actors operate with a theological base, it opens the door for the further theorisation of religion.

The theoretical analysis of mainstream IR has progressed through secularisation thesis but now it has been under scrutiny through various stages. In the first wave of religion and global politics, advocators acknowledged religion and its manifestation in global politics but shelved them as inherited from the earliest human's holdovers of a passed era. Like the myth of the past, religion continued to influence modern secular politics, despite that fact, few people believed in its significant role in contemporary politics. It was actually the theological concepts that became significant in the modern theory of state/states. As Carl Schmitt suggested that not only because of their historical developments in which they were transferred from theology to the theory of the state, whereby, for example, the omnipotent God became the omnipotent lawgiver (Schmitt, 1985).

The example of this debate on how religious legacy continues to shape modern secular politics was Max Weber's linkage of Protestantism and Capitalism. Weber famously argued that the ascetic worldliness of Protestant faith was conducive to many of the values that made for the successful businessman, including restless, continuous, systematic work in a worldly calling (Weber, 1958). While studying Weber's work, David Latin observes in an important review of the first wave that Weber's contribution involved delineation of the ideas of practical religion, and the marshalling of arguments to adduce its economic functions. Latin further observed that Weber constructed the theological, psychological and the sociological components of doctrine together into what Durkheim called the social fact (Latin, 1978). The manifestation of the real world and consequences of religious doctrines was Weber's primary concern (ibid).

Philpott's essay entitled "*The Religious Roots of Modern International Relations*" (2007) is the latest example of this first wave in which he argued that religious ideas are at the roots of modern international relations concluding that had the reformation not occurred, a system of sovereign states would not have developed.

The second wave of theorising religion and international relations focused on contemporary developments and participation by religious actors. Philpott marks the beginning of this wave with the June 1967 Six-Day War between Israel and its Arab neighbours because it signified the beginning of the religion's global resurgence. It awakened a religious conscience among Jews and crippled the prestige of secular nationalism among Arab Muslims (Philpott, 2007). The Israeli occupation of the West Bank and Gaza strip inaugurated a historical shift in Zionism from its secular socialist origin to the increasing predominance of National Orthodox in Israel, with associated implications not only for domestic politics but also for foreign policy (Gorenberg, 2009).

There is a long event in international relations in which religious renaissance played a crucial role. Iranian Revolution of 1978 was another event where religion featured in global politics. To that, we also ought to add the pan-Islamic response to the Soviet invasion of Afghanistan that lead to the rise of fundamentalists movements and formation of ANSA like Al-Qaeda who were the perpetrators of 9/11 attacks. Finally, a host of religiously motivated civil wars broke out in the wake of the Cold War, the most dramatic of which were those in the former Yugoslavia among Latin, Orthodox and Muslim groups. They can most appropriately be characterised as religious wars.

This perceptible augmentation in the frequency of religion affecting international relation encouraged new theorisation of religion and international relations. The most influential example is Samuel P. Huntington's thesis of the Clash of Civilisations. In it, he argued that future global politics would be characterised by the interaction among civilisations, which he defined as the highest cultural grouping whose most common define feature was religion (Huntington, 1993).

With the increased number of religious manifestation in global politics, it gave birth to conceptual changes in the relationship between religion and international relations that set the stage for the third wave of thinking. Part of the momentum for this new thinking was a sequence of developments in global politics where the link between religion and IR was seen in a completely different manner. Here, religion was seen to be deeply infused in political and social elements (Hassner, Omer, Rosato et al, 2012). For example, U.S invasion of Iraq in March of 2003 and subsequent overthrow of Saddam Hussein's Ba'ath regime, a long-term pillar of secular Arab nationalism, was followed by a replacement of that regime, not with another secular democratic one, but by intense religious conflict that ended with the coming to power of a sectarian Shi'a government (ibid).

But it is not just in the Arab World that we see the previously strong walls between politics and religion crumbled. In Turkey, once another epitome of secular nationalism, Kemal Ataturk's Republican Party has been superseded by Islamicist Justice and Development Party (AKP). Episodes in Turkey are not concerning the secular world because it defies one's secular notion of how religion and politics relate to each other. One can see in Turkey's foreign policy the erosion of its relationship with Israel and its newfound commitment to the Palestinian cause, and how the changing role of religion in Turkish politics is affecting regional dynamics. But Turkey is not the only country where the wall of separation between religion and politics is falling down (ibid). The rise of Hindu nationalist BJP in India and the growing influence of its policies by Hindu principles can be taken as an example on how separation between religion and politics is falling down where religion is fused deeply with politics (ibid).

By looking at the waves of theorising religion and IR, it strikes to me that religion does matter in IR. Scholars of IR engrossed in exploring religion and IR need to focus more on middle ground theory than debates on paradigm wars. As Bellin observes that, IR scholars should focus on the variable appeal of transnational religious movements, the variable power of religious ideals to trump material interest, and the variable tendency of religious traditions to inspire violence in international sphere (Bellin, 2008).

The most imperative objective is to understand the cure under-theorisation of religion in IR. First, one needs to identify and separate the effect of various religions, for example separating Islam's effect on ANSA and Christianity's effect on the same (Hassner, Omer, Rosato et al, 2012). Parallel to that is examining the characteristic aspect of religious actors. After having established these things, one needs a theory of religious variation. One also needs a comprehension of how and under what circumstances religion has influence. By carefully examining the debates in the wave of theorising religion and IR, one needs to understand the role of religion in the post 9/11 period.

In the post 9/11 period, ANSA has undergone fundamental changes in opening room for further analysis on theorising religion and IR. The emergence of ISIS is the latest phase of evolution within ANSA. The interpretations that ISIS is making and its wider implications have to be counted as the evidence of the fourth wave and evolution of ANSA. Thus, the main changes that ANSA has undergone after 9/11 consists of two phases. First, is the general evolution into a more networked structure, the greater dispersion of leadership, their recruitment network, weapons, alliances, financial system and control mechanism. ISIS has thus emerged as an updated, new type of transnational ANSA in response to the changing conditions of the international system after 9/11. The interpretation that ISIS was brought within the salafi/jihadist school has instigated the second evolutionary phase for ANSA. In the face of decreasing level interpretation in Al-Qaeda after the death of Osama Bin Laden, the interpretation of Al-Baghdadi, a salafi/jihadist went through a transformational phase in contemporary World politics that has attributed to a violent and terrorist element in ISIS.

The notion of Ummah, something that binds Muslim populations in a metaphysical way has been reinterpreted by ISIS. ISIS structures Ummah model devoted to the caliphate. ISIS calls upon Islam to form a singular global Muslim body while speaking of far-reaching Qur'anic appeals for jihad and the creation of a caliphate. They have designed their interpretation to demarcate boundaries between the in-group and out-group, namely the Muslims belonging to the Ummah of Islam and the Kufr outside of it (Georges, 2015).

The interpretation of Hijrah is stressed by ISIS saying that there is no substitute to Hijrah (emigration) – those who are able must rush to ISIS. Those, however who are capable of emigrating but do not do so will find a place in hellfire. For jihadists, Muslims performing religious rituals without engaging in jihad are fake Muslims (ibid). Principally, Hijrah refers to the journey of Prophet Muhammad and his companions from Mecca to Medina in the course of the first year of the Islamic calendar, in 622 C.E (Esposito, 2003). It also means resistance to colonial rule and the legitimisation of Muslim migration as well as a form of withdrawal from the politics of capitalism, socialism and modernisation/Westernisation (ibid). In a general term, Hijrah refers to the willingness to suffer for faith and the refusal to lose hope in the face of persecution (ibid). One can see how ISIS has used historical Islamic terminology to serve their agenda for magnetising more fighters into ISIS self-proclaimed caliphate.

The number of groups epitomised by a salafi/jihadist school like the groups in Libya, Egypt, Nigeria and others have pledged bayat/alliance with ISIS to help them fight the non-believers. ISIS has asked Muslims all across the globe to perform Hijah, declare bayat and if not both then conduct lone wolf attacks.

ISIS has further used the interpretation of Dar-al-Islam and Dar al-Harb. This inside/outside domain in Islamic interpretation is used by ISIS for their marginalisation policy. Islamic sects refusing to join hand with ISIS in their Global Jihad are considered as outsiders and non-believers of true Islam. Syria and Iraq comprise of various sects within Islam such as Druze, Shia, Yazidi, Kurds etc. ISIS has marginalised these groups using the interpretation from Qur'an by calling them takfirs.

In line with these interpretations, the violent and terrorist element has been attributed. The lone wolf attacks, suicide bombings, beheadings, mass execution, genocide etc. fuelled by ISIS interpretation have all attributed to a violent and terrorist element having a wider implication in world politics.

4.3 ISIS and International Relations

With the advent of ISIS as an ANSA, the international system is being confronted like never before. When ISIS began capturing territories in Iraq and Syria and declared caliphate after capturing Mosul, it rattled European countries and the world. It was for the first time that an ANSA fuelled by radical Islamic ideology declared a caliphate. From its attack to control mechanism, ISIS has dwarfed other ANSA thus bringing a new understanding on how religion has played a significant role in IR that was under-theorised before. ISIS is an evolution within ANSA and one must look at its impact on international relations in order to understand religion's role in the contemporary international system.

4.3.1 Sovereignty and Nation-State System

The understanding of sovereignty still thrives in today's world. Going by the traditional definition of sovereignty, that sovereign, territorially defined states had supreme authority within its borders and a part of world order in which states were the dominant actors (Wickramasinghe, 2015). But the question is whether the state's ability to make an authoritative decision has faded or not; that is, whether the ultimate political authority of the state has shifted to NSA/ANSA or not.

The philosophical influence of religion upon IR is vivid these days on every platform of scholarly debates as witnessed on four waves of theorising religion and IR;

that is, from Max Weber's linkage of Protestantism and Capitalism to the manifestation of ISIS as an ANSA after 9/11 period. ISIS is now dominating the political and geographical landscape in West Asia and their influence has spilt over to other parts of the globe. For a better understanding of ISIS influence on sovereignty and nation-state, one must look at Islamic Sovereignty.

The Islamic ideology emphasises unity among Muslims regardless of social status, ethnicity, race and nationality. Thus, political borders among countries are not recognised by Islam. Islam divides the population into two, Ummah and non-believers. As such, the political loyalty of citizens is not to a state but the Islamic community as a whole (ibid). Having argued about ISIS interpretation on Ummah, it is clear that ISIS believes in Ummah that is bonded in a metaphysical way which travels beyond the boundaries of the nation-state.

ISIS has claimed that the border between Iraq and Syria is now dissolved; they have declared the establishment of a caliphate in the territories it controls in Iraq and Syria. This caliphate impedes upon the customary world order and the system of states as it exists today.

ISIS rejects such a notion of a sovereign state because of religious reasons. There are various religious justifications for ISIS's position, but the common line of argument is that sovereignty for them is a man-made rule that separates all Muslims from each other by man-made borders, therefore recognising is a form of veneration (Wickramasinghe, 2015).

ISIS has been able to mobilise a community of people bound by religious values that exist beyond the territorial boundaries of a state, and in doing so, presents as a substantive, ANSA in a world dominated by nation-state as the primary actors. By mobilising an international community based on religious principles to challenge the domestic politics of states. ISIS border free ambition does not stop there. After declaring caliphate at a Mosque in Mosul on 29th June 2014, ISIS in its self-proclaimed caliph claimed certain region such as Northern and Western part of Africa, former Yugoslavia, Turkey, Afghanistan, Pakistan, Central Asia, West China, Portugal, Spain, France and India were claimed as their mandate and they claimed to establish Sharia law in these territories where Ummah would define the people of these regions ISIS has portrayed Ummah, Global Jihad and Hijrah to magnetise support for their agenda of establishing caliphate and conquering territories in West Asia and beyond to re-establish Sharia law in countries where western form of hierarchical system has taken over (Hosken, 2015). This declaration is contradictory to the sovereign state system. As the U.K. government defines state system as a clearly defined territory with a population, a government who are able of themselves to exercise excessive control of that territory, and independence in their external relations (Shaw, 2008).

The main elements in the Islamic political organisation followed by ISIS that defines state are threefold; the Sharia, the right code of conduct as derived from Qur'an and the Sunnah, the tradition of the Prophet; the caliph as the deputy of the Prophet, the upholder and the executor of Sharia and therefore the chief of legitimacy; and the Ummah. The political tradition relating to the concept of caliphate which developed as a result of this organisational setup, and the Qur'anic requirement of jihad as a collective duty of the Ummah, emphasised euler's authority. Absolutism and unquestioning submission to whoever was in power, irrespective of how he came to acquire it and how he exercised it, came to be supported not only on the ground of the doctrine of necessary, but with reference to the injunctions of the Quran and Hadith of the Prophet (Wickramasinghe, 2015).

ISIS defines sovereignty as absolutism and universal. The conflict for them is not just a matter of survival but the only tool for achieving peace, as there can be no peace without a global political order as brought about essentially through the re-establishment of Islamic State governed by a caliph (Baker, 2005). For them, modernity and western influence have no place in the Islamic world and inclination towards modernity and western influence will not help in establishing a caliphate.

4.3.2 Human Rights

The Preamble to the UN Charter affirms the international legal system's commitment to protecting human rights (Lekas, 2015). The Charter commences:

> *"We the Peoples of United Nations determined to save succeeding generations from the scourge of war…and to reaffirm faith in fundamental human rights."*[72]

In the advancement of its mission to prevent war and protect human rights, the UN adopted several human rights conventions and doctrines (Lekas,2015). In 1948, the Universal Declaration of Human Rights (UDHR) afforded legal recognition to the rights of individuals worldwide (ibid). The Declaration's thirty articles advanced the principle that all humans universally possess inalienable rights (ibid). Article I states:

> *"All human beings are born free and equal in dignity and rights. They are endowed with reason and conscience and should act towards one another in the spirit of Brotherhood."*[73]

The Declaration also proclaims that every human being born worldwide is free and equal. Everyone is entitled to the universal rights set forth in the declaration, regardless of sex, colour, race, language, religion, political or other opinions, national or social origin, property, birth or another status. Principally, everyone has the right to life, liberty and security of person. The UN's desire to prevent religious and political violence is demonstrated in the Declaration's first three articles. The international

---

72 See U.N Charter at http://www.un.org/en/sections/un-charter/preamble/index.html

73 See U.N Declaration of Human Rights at http://www.un.org/en/universal-declaration-human-rights/index.html

community seeks to use universal human rights as a central mechanism in safeguarding peace in the World Legal System. Humans have the right to life and moreover the right to live securely within their territory of origin.[74]

For a long time, IR has been regarded as a playing field for states, where human beings are subordinated to each other through a social contract. The role of human rights in IR, in a very simple phase is to achieve justice. Since there is no definite agreement on what IR perspective holds while measuring human rights, International Law can be used to understand the wider comprehension of human rights from IR perspective. International Law is a core institution in IR representing common values and rules among states.[75] With particular reference to UN Charter, Universal Declaration of Human Rights, International Criminal Tribunal for the Former Yugoslavia (ICTY) etc. it can be argued that commitment to human rights has intensified among states and it is International Law that binds the commitment of the states together. However, state practices and International Law have been relatively weak[76] in terms of translating these ideas in diverse IR reality. The escalation of religiously motivated ANSAs like ISIS and their atrocities against the minorities of captured territories in Iraq and Syria visualises how

---

74 ibid

75 See, https://www.lawteacher.net/free-law-essays/international-law/human-rights-in-international-relations-international-law-essay.php

76 ibid

the implementation of human rights have been proved disastrous. From ISISs strategy of targeting the minorities to their agenda of Global Jihad that has featured beyond West Asia, it is evident that the whole achievement of human rights has been challenged by ANSAs like ISIS having a wider impact on IR.

ISIS's actions evidently violate human rights. Although ISIS rationalises it's doing under the banner of Islam, the group relies on Qur'anic teachings and interpretations to justify their atrocities. Instead, ISIS has disregarded individual's right to life, security, property and executed innocent civilians. The peak of ISIS war crimes can be traced from 2014 when the group began seizing territories. When ISIS swept through northern Iraqi town where Yazidis are concentrated in the region, as many as five thousand Yazidis were executed (Nance, 2016) and five hundred thousand displaced (ibid). Yazidis are not only the minorities targeted by ISIS. Other minorities like Christians, Alawites, Druze, Turkmen, Shia Shabaks and others also fell prey to ISIS atrocities where they were declared as an infidel or takfirs and were sold or executed.

Among the myriads of atrocities committed by ISIS, the issue of rape and slavery may be considered most grievous. For ISIS, rape of captured women is permissible so long as they are considered unbelievers.

Slavery and human trafficking system of ISIS is far reached. ISIS issues official price lists for females, from the ages of one to fifty. Top price goes to younger women, with the value being \$172.[77] Also according to the price list, it is forbidden to purchase more than three slaves unless they are foreigners like Turks, Syrians, and Gulf Arabs.[78] According to a United Nations commission of inquiry report, June 2017, ISIS still holds 3,200 Yezidi women and children (Human Rights Watch, 2017) and such cruelty are a crime against humanity, genocide, war crimes and aggression. Article 4 of the Statute of the International Criminal Tribunal for the Former Yugoslavia (ICTY) defines genocide as:

> *"Genocide means any of the following acts committed with intent to destroy, in whole or in part, national, ethical, racial or religious group, as such: (a) killing members of the group; (b) causing serious bodily or mental harm to members of the group; (c) deliberately deliberately inflicting on group conditions of life calculated to bring about physical destruction in whole or in part; (d) imposing measures intended to prevent births within the group; (e) forcibly transferring children of the group to another group....." (Shaw, 2008; 430).*

ISIS has persecuted and killed people on the basis of their political affiliation, national affiliation, ethnic affiliation and cultural affiliation. The imposition of Sharia law by

---

77 See, UN Official Verified IS Price list for Yazidi and Christian females, 2015. *Defend International.* Accessed November 21, 2017 at http://defendinternational.org/is-price-list-for-yazidi-and-christian-females-verified-by-un-official/

78 ibid

ISIS on seized territories, it displaced the political and civil rights of the people. ISIS has also destroyed the cultural heritage of non-Sunni Muslims. ISIS destroyed Jonah's Tomb, Mosul Central Library, Nimrud, and Tomb of Sheikh Qadeeb Al-Ban Al-Mosuli in Iraq. In Syria, ISIS destroyed Sufi Shrines and City of Palmyra. In response, Irinia Bokova, UNESCO Chief said that ISIS could not silence the history of cultures from the memory of the world (Bokova, 2015).

When the coalition forces started attacking ISIS captured province of Northern Iraq, a series of execution videos followed. On 19th August 2014, ISIS released a video entitled "*Message to America.*(Stern and Berger, 2015)"In this video, James Foley, an American journalist who was kidnapped in Syria was dressed in an orange jumpsuit with his hand tied. A masked ISIS fighter wearing a mask was standing next to him; the fighter beheaded James Foley and said that the life of Americans depends on Obama's next move (Sekulow, 2014). After this, a series of videos were released that showed the execution of aid workers and journalists in the region. Alan Henning and David Hanes, British nationals were also executed by an executioner commonly known as Jihadi John believed to be Mohammed Emwazi from Britain who had joined ISIS. There were other execution videos released under the title *The Resolve of the Defiant* and *Flames of the War,* these videos visualised the execution of Chinese, Russian, Jordanian, Japanese, Norwegian and other nationals (Nance, 2016).

These attempts of ISIS to prevent individuals from practising their profession, religion and culture are in contravention of the Covenant on Civil and Political Rights and the right to self-determination (Lekas, 2015).

ISIS routinely tortures its enemies in violation of International Law. ISIS operates a number of detention facilities within its territory, which it uses to punish those who break Sharia law or oppose ISIS. Many of its prisons are clandestine, and few are known. Known detention centres are in Syria. Individuals suspected of violating Sharia law or oppose ISIS, including children as young as eight years old are abducted and summarily executed in prisons (Sekulow, 2014). Jay Sekulow in his book (2014) *Rise of ISIS: a Threat we cannot ignore* observes *"ISIS violates every single principle of the law of war. (ibid)"* As Article 3 of the laws or customs of war observes that following acts are a violation of jurisdiction:

> *"(a) employment of poisonous weapons or other weapons calculated to cause unnecessary suffering; (b) wanton destruction of cities, towns or villages… (c) attack or bombardment of undefended towns, villages or buildings; (d) seizure of, destruction or wilful damage done to institutions dedicated to religion, charity and education, the arts and sciences, historical monuments and works of art and science; (e) plunder of public or private property…"* (Shaw, 2008; 434).

From ISIS's attacks on holy shrines to execution methodologies, they have violated every aspect of human rights and International Law.

4.3.3 Humanitarian Crisis and Attacks

Syria and Iraq together constitute the worst refugee and displacement scenario in world politics. Since the escalation of the Syrian conflict to the ascent of ISIS, millions have been displaced from their habitat triggering a massive humanitarian crisis that the world has ever seen. Following the humanitarian crisis, ISIS has also managed to attack foreign soil. Countries across the globe are facing new security threats coming from an ANSA. Thus, the whole security dilemma has been reshaped by ISIS.

There are 3.5 million (Smith and Mills, 2015) internally displaced people in Iraq and about 350,000 (ibid) from countries like Syria. An increasing number of Iraqis are fleeing to other countries like Jordan, Turkey etc. Iraq is in increasing danger of suffering and food crisis, as the major agricultural units and lands have been affected by the conflict (ibid). The case is even extreme in Syria as UN Office for Coordination of Humanitarian Affairs estimates that more than 12 million (ibid) Syrians are in need of assistance inside Syria, while more than four million (ibid) have fled to neighbouring countries.

Global forced displacement has increased, with high record numbers. According to the United Nations High Commission of Refugee report 2015–2016, 65.3 million

(UNHCR, 2016) individuals are forcibly displaced worldwide. Out of which 21.3 million (ibid) people are refugees, 40.8 million (ibid) internally displaced people and 3.2 million (ibid) asylum seekers.

The conflict in Syria and Iraq significantly contributed to the rise in the global number of displaced people. By the end of 2016, there was close to 5 million (UNHCR, 2016) Syrian refugee worldwide, an increase of 1 million (ibid) women, men and children within a year. In Syria, Bashar Al-Assad's use of chemical weapons and heavy artillery against its own citizens during the Arab Spring and ISIS escalated the conflict in the region has generated more refugees. The vast majority of these newly displaced populations were registered in Turkey-946,800 (ibid). As a result, Turkey hosted the largest refugees in the globe. Lebanon hosted 1.1 million (ibid) and Jordan 0.6 (ibid) refugees from Syria and Iraq.

Syria and Iraq are not the only countries contributing to worldwide refugee crises. New reignited conflicts in Libya, Nigeria, Afghanistan, Burundi, Yemen, Congo etc. have also contributed to the increase in global displacement crises.

While much of international attention had focused on security threats in West Asia caused by displacement and conflicts, during 2015, another security threat induced by displacement and conflicts affected the immediate region of Europe. A large number of refugees and asylum seekers from Africa, West Asia and Central Asia arrived in Europe. An increasing number of people risked their lives to cross the Mediterranean Sea in search of safety and protection. They crossed the Aegean Sea and landed in Europe and also through the Mediterranean Sea and land routes. Since other countries were reluctant to receiving displaced people, they arrived in Europe. It was estimated that more than 972,551 (Parvathi, 2015) travelled by the Mediterranean Sea and 34,000 (ibid) by land.

European countries were affected by this influx. While many countries were hesitant on allowing the migrants to enter, countries like Greece, Italy and Malta, Spain and Germany allowed these refugees to enter their country. England, Ireland, Scotland and other countries did not allow these migrants to enter. In Greece, 856700(UNHCR, 2016) people were registered, in Italy 153800 (ibid), Malta received 105 (ibid), Spain received 15400 (ibid) and Germany agreed to accept one million refugees, they registered 964574 displaced people.[79]

Conflicts in West Asia, Africa, and Central Asia constituted this global migration crisis. Much of this migration crisis is induced by the Syrian crisis and ISIS but Western countries have also contributed to this crisis. When the coalition force was formed to fight ISIS, it was not only rebel groups and ISIS that became a victim of

---

79 See, Germany Records Largest Influx of Immigrants. Retrieved 24th November 2017 at http://www.dw.com/en/two-million-germany-records-largest-influx-of-immigrants-in-2015/a-19131436

coalition bombings. Civilians in Syria and Iraq were also affected by the coalition force eventually forcing them to leave their country and head towards other neighbouring countries and European region. In this case, even coalition forces have played their part in a migration crisis that engulfed the European region.

Migration crisis is not the only security threat that engulfed the European region. While many migrants were registered, there are thousands of migrants who are not registered. Migrant crisis has proved to be toughest of all. Although governments have already started integrating them, housing, health care, language problem, education etc. will make the government difficult to integrate them. Integrating registered migrants have worked out up to some extent but unregistered migrants have become a threat to the host countries.

Major security threat that the West and other countries witnessed was lone wolf attacks. ISIS agenda of going global meant attacking Western countries in their homeland. After Al-Adnani gave a speech on conducting lone wolf attacks, his motive was to radicalise Muslims living in European countries and beyond. It was an inspiration of terror activities against the West in all parts of the world rather than organising an attack themselves. The message was spread in such a manner that ISIS was able to electrify local residents in the west and instigate them to attack under the banner of jihad. In this way, they would be contributing to the Global Islamic Resistance against the West. As a result of Adnani's instigative speech, lone wolf attacks were witnessed across the globe. These attackers were the one who could neither conduct Hijrah nor declare bayat.

ISIS attack in the West has mostly featured as lone wolf Attack but it has three structures of attacks. This can be looked a little bit further as controlled, guided, networked and inspired. Operatives who are trained in Iraq and Syria and are sent off abroad with specific instructions and resources on targets are controlled. These operatives also remain in significant contact with ISIS. Guided are those who receive an endorsement to carry out an attack under ISIS banner. These operatives travel to an area controlled by ISIS where they would get broad outlines of an attack. ISIS does this with the help of Amn al-Kharji (ISIS foreign intelligence service). Lastly, inspired are those who carry out the attack with their own plan without any assistance of Amn al-Kharji and ISIS. This is the true category of lone wolf. Those individuals who act as a lone wolf are most difficult to stop because of their self-preparation without any contact with ISIS.

ISIS attacks are the most lethal security threat that the West has ever witnessed. Most of their attacks took off against the West. For instance, the Charlie Hebdo massacre in France killed 12(Henry Jackson Society, 2017), the Paris attack on November 2015 killed 130 (ibid). France witnessed 20 (ibid) ISIS attacks, the US witnessed 16 (ibid), Germany witnessed 12 (ibid), Britain witnessed 8 (ibid) and Belgium 7 (ibid). ISIS threat was also felt in countries like Australia where the country witnessed 9 (ibid). Other countries have also been a victim of ISIS attack.

It was evident from 2014 onwards that new security threat has emerged in IR driven by ANSA with radical Islamic interpretation. To combat security threats like humanitarian crisis, human rights violation, non-conventional attack on foreign soil etc. triggered by an ANSA. Countries have come together to form a coalition for self-defence against ISIS and humanitarian intervention.

4.4 Coalition Contribution to Countering ISIS

In terms of Counter-ISIS coalition mandate, United Nations Security Council (UNSC) passed several resolutions such as 2170, 2178 and 2199 to make a call on member states to take assorted steps to include coalition strategy such as humanitarian relief, countering terrorist financing and counter ISIS managing strategy. According to the United Nations Charter, Article 2(4) prohibits the use of force against internal sovereignty of state/s. Even though ISIS commits gross human rights violations, triggers a humanitarian crisis and threatens the existence of the state system, the theory of humanitarian applies only to state/s. The action to combat ISIS is neither action against state actors, nor it is aimed to overthrow the existing Syrian government, rendering the theory of humanitarian intervention a non-viable justification to infringing on Syria's territorial boundaries (Lekas, 2015).

In order to execute the coalition mandate, coalition participants have cited the Iraqi Government's letter to the UNSC requesting defence assistance and stating that Iraq faces threats from ISIS in Syria as a further legal basis for participating in the military coalition (Mcinnis, 2016). Obama Administration maintained that it has legal authorisation for a military intervention through 2001 and 2002 Iraq Resolution. But their main interest was to stop security threat posed by ANSAs and for the regional hegemonic position.

On September 10, 2014, President Obama announced the formation of a global coalition to defeat ISIS. Subsequently, over sixty nations (John, 2014) and partner organisations agreed to participate, contributing either military forces or resources (or both) to the campaign. In Brussels in 2014, countries agreed to organise and support the coalition mandate. They agreed to support military operations, capacity building and training, stop the flow of foreign terrorist fighters, cut off ISIS financial network; address humanitarian relief and crises, and expose ISIS true nature (ibid). The military component of the coalition to defeat ISIS began its *"operation inherent resolve"* (Mcinnis, 2016) soon after countries agreed to cooperate and fight against their common enemy.

According to the United States Central Command and open source reporting, around twenty-seven countries (Cronk, 2016) have agreed to join the coalition with an objective of destroying ISIS and homeland protection. Accordingly the campaign has three primary military components: coordinated air strikes, training and equipping local security forces and special target operations, some based on Northen Iraq while others dedicated to operating in Syria (Starr, 2016).

According to the Department of Defense, as of June 2016, the coalition conducted 13,470 airstrikes and 26374 targets were destroyed.[80] Operation Inherent Resolve seemed successful initially with 66 (Mcinnis, 2016) participant countries contributing to the coalition financially and militarily as decided during the NATO summit where 10[81] countries had decided to fight ISIS militarily through air support and supplies. However, towards the end of 2015, coalition countries were facing numerous obstacles.

Despite the expenditure of $500 million (Mcinnis, 2016), the coalition proved unable to counter ISIS

---

80 See, U.S Department of Defense. 2016. Operation Inherent Resolve: Targeted Operations against ISIL Terrorists. Retrieved, 26th November 2017, at http://www.defense.gov/News/Special-Report/0814_Inherent-Resolve

81 "Secretary of State John Kerry urged France, UK, and others to support the fight against the Islamist group in Iraq," Time, December 15 2015, http://time.com/3273185/isis-us-nato/

financial mechanisms. ISIS has demonstrated a degree of strategic level reach. ISIS captured the city of Ramadi, the provincial capital of al-Anbar, after a long struggle. Ramadi constitutes the majority Sunni population which is favourable to ISIS. The city is also crucial for control over Anbar province and for towns along the Euphrates River leading to al-Raqqa, the ISIS centre of operations in Syria. The city is just 60km from Baghdad. After successfully capturing Ramadi, ISIS eyed for Kobane but they were driven out by Kurdish forces. When the coalition had focused on retaking Mosul (Islamic Caliphate of ISIS), ISIS captured Palmyra that led the coalition to shift their focus from Mosul operation to Palmyra and Ramadi. Palmyra occupation seemed significant for ISIS because of rich gas reserves and classical antiquities, giving ISIS leverage and money. The greatest challenges to the coalition were ISIS strategy of resupplying its troops and war machines across Iraq and Syria from Abu Kamel, confronting the coalition force on the battlefield. ISIS has also demonstrated its global reach by attacking western cities, notably Paris, Brussels and others.

ISIS flourishes in the absence of a strong and unified state response. ISIS has dodged state persecution, even from the Syrian regime. Most of the state persecution on ISIS has been in the form of airstrikes and military assistance in Iraq and de-facto region of Kurdistan (Klausen, 2015). On the other hand, with the international coalition against ISIS, the group seems to have unleashed a new wave of religion impact on IR. Unlike the Al-Qaeda related attacks, ISIS attack seems to be more of religious form. Such religiously motivated attacks were seen in Paris, Charlie Hebdo massacre etc. ISIS has proven particularly adept at using weaknesses in the state system, they have radicalised youths in western land encouraging them to attack just by giving a hate speech against the West. Such strategies have compelled states to penetrate into ISIS modus operandi system to track down the recruiters and instigators of global attacks. But the coalition has failed to do so because of their regional interest in West Asia.

For instance, the coalition force is led by the US with sixty countries (Smith and Mills, 2015) assisting to counter ISIS advancement. The United Kingdom, Australia, France, Belgium, Denmark, Jordan and Netherland and Gulf countries have all conducted air strikes against ISIS. Canada initially was a coalition ally but after Justin Trudeau came to power, he was reluctant to involve Canada against ISIS. However, these countries seem to have their own interest in their sleeves.

It is for the first time that a coalition is formed to skirmish ANSAs. The concept of the Westphalian system (understand that has dominated IR thinking), over the last two decades faced many challenges due to the escalation of NSA/ANSAs. This effect is felt in West Asia more so than anywhere else. The Westphalian notion of the nation-state is, in themselves, an alien concept to religiously driven ANSAs like ISIS, where God/Allah is considered to be the embodiment of universal sovereignty. With the advent of ISIS and the proclamation of the new caliphate, the hegemony of Westphalian authority is confronted like never before. In the post 9/11 period, IR is moving beyond Westphalian understanding which will take decades to understand.

4.4.1 U.S.A.

U.S.A continues to lead the different coalition forces conducting airstrikes against ISIS (ibid) they have struck the major cities in Syria and Iraq that have come under ISIS control. The US have been bolstering Kurdish forces, and training Iraqi forces and Turkish moderates with weapons and money. They have deployed 450 personnel (ibid) and counting US troops to advise the forces fighting ISIS in the region. The $500 million (ibid) programme has been approved for assisting ground forces skirmishing ISIS. With its $500 million (ibid) programme, US has also assisted groups like Free Syrian Army (FSA), Jaish al-Nasr, Victory of the Oppressed, Eastern Ghouta Unified Command, One Flag Alliance, Qalamoun, Southern Front and Jaysh al-Harmoun to fight against ISIS and Basher Al-Assad. The United States' main motive in the region is to regain its control over countries by establishing regimes inclined towards the West and Democratic Regimes. U.S.A is more inclined on toppling Assad so they have been funding these groups to fight

Assad regime, U.S.A is focused more on fighting Assad and bring Democracy in Syria to stabilise the region with democratic regimes or friendly regimes.

After Donald Trump won the presidential election, things have turned out in a different way. Following his inauguration in January 2017, Donald Trump stated that defeating and destroying ISIS and other radical Islamic groups will be their highest priority (Smith and Mills, 2017). He also signed a memorandum saying that ISIS would be defeated in 30 days. US is now focused on driving out ISIS from their strategic locations by helping the Syrian Democratic Force with ammunitions and finance. US has also been helping Iraqi forces with advisers and personnel to conduct a ground strike against ISIS

4.4.2 Russia

Russia rolled its dice in the Syrian conflict on 30th September 2015. It is for the first time that Russian forces have undertaken a military operation beyond Europe after 1979. Initially, Russian air strikes targeted anti-Assad forces that were funded by the U.S.A. and ISIS. Russian entry into the Syrian conflict became a game changer. Syria gives its geographic space to Russia where Latakia became Russia's air base and Tartus, which is on the southern part of Latakia became a naval base for Russia. Since then Russia has increased the number of aircraft and marines. Russia collaborated with Assad and Hezbollah forces to conduct a military campaign against ISIS. However, on October 31, 2015, when the Russian Metrojet Flight 9268 was downed over Sinai by ISIS,[82]Russia shifted its focus to ISIS.

Although, Russia has actively participated in fighting ISIS, it has a long-term strategy in the region. Russia has only two allies in West Asia; Iran and Syria. If the Syrian regime topples then Russian engagement in the region will diminish. Russia denies the fact that Bashar al-Assad is their main concern. However, they are concerned about the Syrian regime. Moscow is also eyeing increased trade and economic opportunities with Syria after the conflict (Smith and Mills, 2015). With Syria and Iran are only allies remaining in West Asia, Russia aims to maintain its influence in West Asia.

Russian President Vladimir Putin announced on March 14, 2016, that Russia would begin withdrawing the main part of its forces from Syria. Observers subsequently noted that this did not indicate a full withdraw from Syria. Most recently, Russia has also reportedly launched airstrikes in Syria from Iranian territory (Cunningham and Deyoung, 2016).

---

82   See, ISIS Planned to Attack Israeli Vessels After Commandeering Egyptian Missile Boat. *Algemeiner.* Retrieved, 28th November, 2017. At, http://www.algemeiner.com/2014/12/01/isis-planned-to-attack-israeli-vessels-after-commandering-egyptian-missile-boat/

After Donald Trump took over the US presidency, Russia and the US have shown willingness to work together for skirmishing ISIS and other ANSA in the region. While the Astana arrangements have failed to address key issues in West Asia, the fact that the Trump Administration sending an envoy to Russia on May 2017 may signal U.S.A. willingness to work with Moscow. The alleged use of chemical weapons in April 2017 by the Syrian government, after a commitment by the Russians to organise their disposal, would be an example of Russia's failure to deliver the Syrians (Smith and Mills, 2017).

4.4.3 Iran and Saudi Outlook

Iran also shares the same interest as Russia does, Syria is Tehran's only ally in West Asia. Iran has been supporting Assad from the inception of the crises, at the same time they have helped Syria with Shiite militants to counter ISIS and anti-regime factions. Assad regime in Syria, is extremely valuable to Iran. Iran has been perhaps the major supporter of the Syrian government in the conflict, supported overtly by the Lebanese Hezbollah force (Claire and Mills, 2015). Iran is a significant player in West Asia having acquired a large amount of different missiles, from short range to long-range missiles like Soumar, Fateh, Shahab etc. These missile programmes of Iran are to counter regional power like Saudi Arabia. Saudi Arabia and Iran are the two superpowers of West Asia. And both the countries have been trying to spread their influence in the region.

The power struggle between the two axes was seen during regional proxy wars. Iran has been funding the Hezbollah forces in Lebanon and Houthi rebels in Yemen to counter anti-Shiite forces designed by Saudi Arabia. For Iran, their major interest lies in establishing a Shia regime in the region, Saudi Arabia looks to strengthen Sunni majority in the region. This clash of interest between Iran and Saudi Arabia lies in their ideological foundation. Saudi Arabia is the architect of Wahhabi movement that has been wielded by various ANSA in the region, similarly Iran has ideological linage with Hezbollah, Hamas and Houthi. The antagonism between the two has now become a geopolitical struggle. In this case, the Assad regime becomes a significant bridge for Iran to retain Hezbollah in Lebanon and losing Assad would make a bad cost for Iran. On the other hand, Saudi Arabia is funding anti-Assad ANSA to establish a friendly regime in Syria.

The antagonism between Tehran and Riyadh is deeply knotted with regional geopolitics. Saudi Arabia has been supporting Sunni ANSA in Syria whereas Iran shares ideological linage with Hezbollah and other groups. However, after Russian involvement in such geopolitical enigma things are moving towards Iranian side as they have captured major cities from ISIS stronghold and from Iraqi side also Shiite militants are playing a prominent role in driving ISIS from their stronghold positions.

In May 2017, Hassan Rouhani was re-elected with 57% (Claire and Mills, 2017) of the vote. Rouhani's coming back to power clearly signals that Iran would prioritise to establish a corridor through Syria and Iraq easing Iranian support to Assad and Hezbollah forces.

4.4.4 Turkey

Turkey has been acting like an awkward ally to the West and NATO forces. Turkey has opened borders where ISIS and other ANSA have been moving freely and weapons have been exchanged through illicit trade in the region of Kilis and Cobanbey. Turkey has not allowed American drones to fly in these regions. Turkey's main motive is to avoid any direct confrontation between NATO and ISIS but bringing direct confrontation between the Americans and Assad's force would help Turkey retain its geographical location which Kurds have asked for an independent region. Turkey's major strategy is to prevent Kurdistan region autonomy. Kurds have claimed the southern region of Turkey in their autonomy region threatening Turkey's existing geographical space.

The expansion of ISIS in the Kobane region would eliminate PKK and the Kurdish population and this is what Turkey is waiting for. The downing of Russian air fighter on the Turkish border is also because of their hesitant policy and self-interest as once the Russian set their foot on Suruc region then the assistance to Kurds will increase from the Russian font too. US have already supplied the Kurds with war machines to fight ISIS Turkey does not want another big power politics to come to play in their geographic space which will hamper their self-interest.

A July 2016 failed coup in Turkey have raised questions about Turkish military capabilities and morale, as well as U.S/NATO-Turkey dynamics that could affect future coalition use of Turkish bases and other aspects of Turkey's participation in the anti-IS coalition (Mcinnis, 2016).

4.4.5 Kurds

Kurds remain predominant actor in both Syria and Iraq. YPG forces, close to the terrorist-designated PKK of Turkey have been essential to military successes against ISIS in places such as Kobane, near Syria's border with Turkey (Smith and Mills, 2017). But that triggered a yet more problematical scenario in the conflict, as Turkey's contribution has progressively wrought by hostility to YPG and the PKK in the light of the Turkish government. However, Kurds have benefitted with U.S entry on war, as the U.S has been supporting them with arms and finance to eliminate ISIS and in doing so, Kurds demand of an Independent Kurdistan would be actualised.

4.4.6 France

France is active in the region fighting ISIS wholeheartedly; especially after the Paris attack Hollande has focused more on air strikes to eliminate the financial networks of ISIS since France is a most affected country where major attacks have taken a voyage on its geographic space. This has increased concern among the *Schengen* countries where strict border check is being placed among these countries to avoid radicalism inflow from the Balkans and Brussels to other countries. European countries since then have been supporting the cause and fight against ISIS where France is mostly involved. Now that Emmanuel Macron has taken over, the French role in the coalition can shift because of crises that the country is facing at home.

4.4.7 Syria

Bashar al-Assad has benefitted from the on-going war; first Russia has come to its rescue and U.S funded rebels have been bombarded by Russia; second the growth of ISIS will shift the focus of rebel group fighting him to ISIS so there are chances for him to stay in power in upcoming years. There are lesser chances of stripping Assad from his powers. Russia and Syrian forces have been playing a significant role in fighting ISIS strongholds in Palmyra, Raqqa and Aleppo. ISIS rebels have been driven out from these cities. Now, ISIS holds Deir ez-Zor, al-Mayadin and Abu Kamal in Syria.

4.4.8 Iraq

The fate of Iraq's third city, Mosul;\ has dominated Iraqi political scene since 2014 when it fell to ISIS (ibid).

However, after Haider al-Abadi became the President of Iraq, Iran started backing Shiite militias to fight ISIS. Shiite militias are advancing towards ISIS occupied cities like Falluja and Mosul. Haider al-Abadi has officially recognised Shiite militias. The Shiite militias (PRF) have become central to the future of Iraq, the group has driven out ISIS from major parts of Fallujah and Mosul which could not be achieved by US-led air strikes. Increasingly, ISIS is being squeezed into a ribbon along the Euphrates valley. Having lost the Iraqi city of Mosul and on the retreat in the Syrian city of Raqqa, their last redoubt is likely to be the province of Abu Kamal. There too ISIS is vulnerable from both sides. From western side Assad force along with Russian are likely to expand further and from the Eastern side Shiite militants and Iraqi army are moving further. ISIS black flag has been lowered in Mosul (ISIS caliphate). ISIS just holds the western front of Iraqi border with Syria.

4.5 Future of ISIS

Neutralisation of ISIS leaders and shrinking of the territory has now put a question to what would be the future of ISIS. ISIS has lost its major occupied cities like Mosul, Aleppo, Fallujah, Tikrit and other significant provinces that have reduced ISIS financial mechanisms and military. ISIS generates its revenue with taxes, oil, kidnappings etc. losing ground in Syria and Iraq has diminished ISIS both militarily and financially.

However, ISIS thrives on the weak state system. Iraq and Syria are strengthened with coalition forces and once the coalition fighting force withdraws from Iraq and Syria, ISIS could regain its strength. Long-term guerrilla campaigns could continue in Iraq and Syria because the group is still present in sparsely populated desert areas (Smith and Mills, 2017).

ISIS could still gain strength because of failure of Shia led government of Iraq to rebuild liberated areas, or to reintegrate Sunni populations into its political system. In cities like Mosul and Fallujah, unemployment is sky high and the echoes of de-baathification policy that alienated Sunnis is still felt. ISIS can increase its military strength because of state failure to integrate these isolated Sunni populations.

Sunni leaders in Karmah has felt that Iraq is increasing ties with hard-line Shia theocracy next door and the government in Iraq is more focused on working with Shia militias than helping Sunnis rebuild. This in turn could favour ISIS because ISIS feeds on marginalised Sunni populations. In fact, ISIS captured major cities in Iraq and Syria with the help of marginalised Sunnis who were isolated from government schemes. Isolation of Sunnis at the hands of Iraqi politics will be a boon to ISIS. ISIS has also learnt from its shrinking position currently, this will help ISIS to evolve into a stronger ANSA with better modus operandi system.

ISIS leaders and fighters have dispersed to other provinces of Egypt, Libya, Afghanistan, Yemen etc. all have areas held by ANSA that have pledged bayat with ISIS. Those provinces could strengthen ISIS global outreach. The recent attack on Egypt that killed around 230 people (Lee and Spark, 2017) signifies that ISIS can operate from its affiliated provinces. After Mosul fell under ISIS, various ANSA from West Asia, Central Asia, Caucasus, Africa etc. had pledged an alliance with ISIS. Now that ISIS is on the losing ground, these ANSA affiliated to ISIS has expanded from their provinces.

ISIS has already radicalised foreign nationals and encouraged them to conduct lone wolf attacks. European countries have faced lone wolf attacks recently in London Bridge etc. ISIS sympathisers and fighters have returned to their home countries and these fighters could mount an attack under the banner of ISIS.

In Syria, Russia and Assad forces along with Hezbollah have allowed ISIS to flee. These ISIS fighters have entered deserted provinces of Northern and Eastern Syria. It is likely that these fighters can operate from their clandestine bases under the command of Abi Bakr Al-Baghdadi.

ISIS has spread messages to their affiliated bodies across the globe to continue skirmish Western countries. These ISIS-affiliated ANSAs have also declared Global Jihad against the West. This is a clear indication that attacks under the banner of Islam will feature across the globe. Moreover, ISIS has been pushed to the edge and not completely destroyed as it still holds territory in Abu Kamel, Dier ez-Zor, al-Mayadin and other villages in Syria and Iraq. ISIS can radicalise isolated Sunnis from their thriving position. And once the coalition forces vacate from West Asia then it will leave room for ISIS to expand from their clandestine bases and affiliated provinces.

4.6 Conclusion

ISIS efforts to keep up their search for new vulnerabilities in the state system and new patterns of waging war is one of the primary reasons why the interaction with the enemy leads to further expansion of transnational space making a big impact on IR. ANSAs have the most compelling motivation to invent new ways of conflictive interactions with the state. For instance, the violation of human rights and war crimes committed during the time of conflict. They find a new place of vulnerability in the state system. ANSAs invent a new way of attacking state as one has seen how ANSAs like ISIS have conducted their attack strategies on western soil triggering massive humanitarian crises. The state system responds either to block ANSAs way by forming a coalition among the state system. For instance, ISIS spillover effect and their ways of manipulation and attacks have forces countries to form an alliance to skirmish the group.

In the case of ANSAs such as ISIS, who are religiously motivated, interaction with the state will create a precarious situation where religion becomes a driving force of such conflicts. ISIS is a product of post 9/11 evolution within ANSAs, and ISIS is constantly inventing and exploring new ways and places to attack as seen during Paris attacks, and thereby provoking counter-responses from the state system. The key issues of the international system itself, such as hegemony, sovereignty, humanitarian laws, human rights etc. have all been challenged and changed post 9/11 because of religiously motivated ANSAs. It is evident that religion will dominate and will trigger international conflicts.

Conclusion

The argument of this book has been that the study of IR was governed by state-centric paradigms and the comprehension of the discourse had been in a single dimension where relation among states was the primary focus. It was with the epistemological inquiry of theories like Critical Theory, constructivism, feminism etc. which brought a new debate in understanding IR integrating other actors and challenges in the inquiry of IR. During this transformational phase, state-centric theories were challenges since they were not able to integrate other actors in the comprehension of IR.

It is evident that IR witnessed significant changes after the end of the Cold War. End of the Cold War visualised paradigm shift leading to the emergence of new actors in IR. In such myriad of complexity, Non-State Actors (NSA) emerged as a significant player in IR. IR theories have traditionally been biased to understanding the overarching structure of IR. With the increased involvement of NSAs, IR theories were not able to comprehend this shift in their theoretical consideration. In such bewilderment, Theory of Open Source Anarchy

(OSA) explicates that anarchy, which is a closed concept in IR where only states participated, have now become open making room for NSA and Armed Non-State Actors (ANSA) penetration. Theory of OSA has unambiguously integrated NSA/ANSAs into their analysis.

The balance between NSAs and states has altered over the past 30–40 years. It is lucid that NSA/ANSAs took centre stage on the facet of globalisation and inflated after the end of the Cold War. The idea of transnationalism has come back with an increase in the involvement of NSAs and its materialisation into ANSAs. NSAs like IGOs, INGOs, MNCs, Humanitarian and Religious Organisations etc. have increased involved in IR over the past decades. However, there is an intricacy in defining NSAs. There are NSAs that are fully autonomous such as armed groups operating in a transnational manner etc. there are NSAs that are fully semi-autonomous and operates with state/states assistance (banks, NGOs, MNCs etc.) whereas some are considered a threat by state/states (Hezbollah, Boko Harem, Al-Qaeda etc.). Clear concepts have not been laid down in understanding NSAs.

Researchers have overlooked the broader understanding of NSAs where threat perception has shifted towards NSAs and within NSAs, it has further shifted towards ANSAs. It was during the 9/11 period or after 9/11 number of works appeared that dealt with violent non-state actors (VNSA) or ANSA. Scholars like

Oliver Roy (2002), Rohan Gunaratna (2002), Steve Coll (2008), Michael Scheurer (2004), Ersel Aydinli (2016), David P Fidler (2008), Peter G. Thomson (2014) et al. have provided further analysis on ANSAs or VNSAs. At their most basic level, ANSAs operates within the state system, they are characterised as violent groups primarily motivated by ideology and political goals. For instance, ANSAs like de-facto Governing Authorities in Kurdistan, National Liberation Movements (NLMs) in Palestine, Transnational Criminal Organisation (TCOs) in Mexico and Columbia, Non-State Armed Groups like Uyghur Liberation Organisation, Jeemah Islamiyah etc. can be considered as most autonomous ANSAs operating within states but away from state/states influences.

ANSAs include all armed groups in comprehending typologies which is in a way very contested. For instance, there are groups that are politically motivated and supported by state/states, this includes groups like Hezbollah, Taliban, Houthi Rebels etc. some are ideologically and theologically motivated e.g.: ISIS, Al-Qaeda, Jeemah Islamiyah etc. Therefore there is a problem in understanding ANSAs and its transnationalism and non-statehood. In order to disentangle such bewilderment, autonomy, representation and influence (ARI) framework have been used.

The argument among the scholars in understanding transnationalism and non-statehood of revolutionary/ Ideologically and theologically driven ANSAs are to disentangle how such ANSAs are confined with a particular ideology. As discussed in chapter two, it is apparent that Islam has travelled in a transnational manner through interpretations. Islamic scholars like Ibn Tayimmah, Ibn al-Wahhab, Jamal ad-din al-Afghani, Mohammad Abduh, Syed Qutb, Syed Abul al Mawdudi et al. contributed to three distinctive ideology of Islam (traditional, non-traditional and jihadi/salafi) that has become defining components of ANSAs ideological base. Major questions addressed in this study are: How political instability in West Asia triggered the growth of ISIS as an ANSA? What has been the impact of ISIS in IR? Chapter 2 and chapter 5 addressed these questions. The discussions are comprehended below. ISIS as a focus of my study, its ideological base lies in the interpretation of jihadi/salafi school and has a long evolutionary history starting from the Soviet intervention of Afghanistan to Arab Spring, ISIS was able to exploit state vulnerabilities in Iraq and Syria. The rampant expansion of ISIS gained glare of publicity in IR on 29th June 2014 when Abu Bakr Al-Baghdadi was declared as a new Caliph Ibrahim in a Mosque in Mosul after they topped regime forces in the city (Stern and Berger, 2015). ISIS claimed to establish an Islamic State and called out to Muslims across the globe for Hijrah and join ISIS for Global Jihad. ISIS aims to restore Islamic jurisprudence by employing strict Sharia law to expand its legitimacy across the globe.

ISIS has become one of the most organised ANSA with proper *modus operandi* and strategy. ISIS has an appropriately organised hierarchical system where members under these councils help the group to carry out its operations in West Asia and beyond. ISIS has derived its strength by recruiting foreign fighters. ISIS is considered the world's best-financed ANSAs due to the cash and natural resources they possess from international donors, taxation and extortion, kidnappings and looting, oil trade etc. earning 1.5 million (Johny, 2015) a day. ISIS is also using sophisticated war machines to carry out their propaganda of establishing an Islamic State. They have seized sophisticated weapons from captured territories. Their arsenals have increased over a period time possessing weapons like Howitzers, Humvees etc.

The spill over effect has come to play in understanding the expansion of ANSAs in IR and ISIS in particular. Several other ANSAs operating in other parts of the world have declared an alliance with ISIS. Groups in Egypt, Algeria, Nigeria etc. having pledged an alliance with ISIS shows the extensiveness of ISIS in IR. ISIS voyage on foreign soil and the way ISIS is bringing new methodology to communicate with the West has visualised ISIS effect in IR.

ISIS is a religiously motivated ANSA that has the salafi/jihadi element in it. As illustrated in chapter four, religion is an under-theorised concept in IR. With the advent of ISIS in post 9/11 period, it has opened the door for the further theorisation of religion in IR. From ISIS's violation of human rights to challenging the Westphalian notion of nation-state, ISIS has further opened the door for analysis on how religion is shaping IR.

The main purpose of this topic *"Armed Non-State Actors in International Relations: A study on ISIS"* was to provide a comprehension on how power is shifting from state/states to NSAs and how ANSAs are playing a prominent role in IR. While previous works of literature have provided significant ideas on categorising ANSAs and their co-relation with the state system, but they are inadequate when endeavouring to access theologically motivated ANSAs like ISIS. Islamic ideological base framework comprehended in chapter two is specifically aimed at scrutinising how Islamic interpretation contributed to motivating ANSAs like ISIS, Boko Harem etc. through its interpretations. Similarly in Chapter one, ARI framework is used to understand the autonomy of ANSAs that attracts various theoretical considerations leading to a cobweb paradigm in understanding ANSAs. By using these frameworks (Islamic ideological base and ARI), previous chapters have comprehended the possibility of comparing and analysing various ANSAs like ISIS.

A significant implication of the ARI framework is exhibiting the interaction between ISIS and IR. It also scrutinises non-statehood of ISIS. The autonomy of any ANSAs can be looked from the spectrum whether it is distant from the state and state-centric regime or not. In the case of ANSAs like ISIS, it has kept itself distant from the state. ISIS has not used the state as a support system for financial aid and infrastructure. They have used the state's territory as a base for fighting after capturing provinces like Mosul, Anbar etc. but ISIS has kept itself aloof from the state support system. ISIS has explored their financial background. As discussed in chapter three, ISIS financial mechanism consists of taxation, looting, oil trade etc. that are seized from the state/states. While using their financial background, ISIS has survived state/ states repressive policy. ISIS comes under the active categorisation of ANSAs where they have defended themselves from state/states forces while manipulating weaknesses of state-centric regimes in order to ease their own functioning.

ISIS is religiously and ideologically defined when it comes to representation. ISIS is not confined to Muslims for recruitment. They have recruited fighters of all faith. It was after these fighters reached Iraq and Syria they converted to Muslims. They are more focused on achieving their dream of establishing an Islamic State across the globe. This has led to outstretch of ISIS in IR where various groups from Libya, Nigeria, Algeria, Egypt, Indonesia etc. have pledged an alliance with ISIS. These groups or sub-groups of ISIS have an agreed agenda of establishing an Islamic State and targeting the infidels.

ISIS has global transformative influence threatening state capacities. They have exploited state spectrum of strong and weak capabilities. ISIS attacks on foreign lands, their recruitment strategy of influencing foreign youths for Hijrah, organised modus operandi system etc. has visualised the transformative capacity of ISIS. The result, as Aydinli observes that state/states behaviour changes with ANSAs act in IR then that particular ANSA can be said to be the most influential actor in IR (Aydinli, 2016). ISIS has changed the security dilemma in IR by violating human rights and triggering massive humanitarian crises, making European countries the victim of its atrocities. As a response to ISIS's act, countries have formed an alliance to skirmish the group. The wave of ISIS influence has rattled foreign countries forcing them to form an alliance. This has changed the environment of IR urging countries to shift their focus from domestic dynamic to ISIS. It can therefore be said that ISIS transformative strategies have increased ISIS's influence. After having measured ISIS under the framework of ARI, it is lucid that ISIS has emerged as the most autonomous ANSA dwarfing other ANSAs.

The theoretical framework of the study started with the Theory of Open Source Anarchy (OSA) by Fidler. OSA posit that, anarchy, which is a closed system in IR where only states participate has now become open making it easy for NSA/ANSAs to penetrate. When anarchy becomes visible for NSA/ANSAs to penetrate, then the whole power structure will shift. Such a shift in power from states to NSA/ANSAs has featured in the past several decades. As discussed in chapter one of the study, power is shifting geographically and from statist to non-statist. The second shift is more transformative because new players have emerged and increased their transnationalism in polity shift.

While conceptualising polity shift, it has transformed through persuasion, trust and apathy. Transformation taking place through persuasion and trust are created by state/states, while transformation through apathy occurs when the state becomes weak and NSA/ANSAs takes over. The escalation of ISIS has featured because of apathy where state/states have become weak or unable to address the political and economic requirements. Such transformation through apathy has engulfed the whole Middle East and North Africa (MENA) region where various ANSAs have emerged challenging the legitimacy of the nation-state. Groups like Salafist Group for Preaching and Combat, Al-Qaeda, Hamas, Hezbollah, Fath al-Islam etc. have emerged challenging state legitimacy. Due to the increasing number of ANSAs, a power transfer from states to ANSAs are happening that makes ANSAs the rivals of states. It can be traced in the strengthening of the capacity of influence or the growing number of interactions. The study has proved that ANSAs are able to act as rivals in the monopoly of violence.

With the advent of ISIS as an ANSA, stage in the evolution within ANSAs are taking place. ANSAs have now started acting like a state by taking responsibilities to operate better and use their economy is an efficient manner. As discussed in chapter four, the evolution within ANSAs has featured with the rise of ISIS which is more networked and properly structured compared to other ANSAs. ISIS escalation and their methodologies of manipulation and Islamic interpretation have brought in an evolutionary trend within a salafi/jihadi school. Their interpretation of Global Jihad, Hijrah, caliphate, Ummah etc. have featured in assorted ways. They have applied ijtihad for waging war against the west and establishing an Islamic State. Expanding the political space of state/states, ISIS has grown and evolved to be the most formidable ANSA epitomised by the jihadi/salafi school. Contemplating ISIS's evolution in IR, it is apparent that religion theorisation of IR is possible.

ISIS is a religiously motivated ANSA that has a salafi/jihadi element in it. As illustrated in chapter four, religion is an under-theorised concept in IR. Scholars have often been misled by secularisation thesis that holds that religion does not have any role to play in IR. However, scholars like Monica Duffy (2012), Eva Bellin (2001), Samuel P. Huntington (1993), Sebastian Rosato (2012) et al. showed ways for theorising religion in IR. With the advent of ISIS in post 9/11 period, it has opened the door for the further theorisation of religion in IR. From ISIS's violation of human rights to challenging the Westphalian notion of nation-state, ISIS has opened the door for analysis on how religion is shaping IR.

The larger intellectual takeaways from the three waves of theorising religion in IR seem to be simply summarised as the gradual decline of secularism in IR (Hassner, Omer, Rosato et al, 2012). The most recent wave of theorising religion and IR was actualised by the escalation of ISIS opening door for reformation of IR.

References

Ahmad, Talmiz. (2005), *Reform in the Arab World: External Influences and Regional Debates,* New Delhi: Indian Research Press.

Alami Mina. (2014), Women on the front lines, *NOW.* Accessed, Nov 17, 2016. At: http://now.mmedia.me//ib/en/reportsfeatures/535456-women-on-the-front-

Alami, Mina. (2014), Women on the front lines, *NOW.* Accessed, Nov 17, 2016. At: http://now.mmedia.me//ib/en/reportsfeatures/535456-women-on-the-front-lines

Alaneme Justina, Egesi Canon. (2015), Islamic State of Iraq and Syria-A Threat to Global Peace and Security. *IOSR Journal of Business and Management.* Volume 17, Issue I. Ver III, PP 45–49.

Alessandra, Masi. (2015), Al-Qaeda, ISIS Cooperate in Lebanon, But that's just a Temporary Tactic. *International Business Times.* Accessed, Dec 11, 2015. At: http://www.ibtimes.com/al-qaeda-isis-cooperation-lebanon-thats-just-temporary-tactic-1828258?rel=rel2

Al-Ghoul. (2014), Gaza Salafists pledge Allegiance to ISIS. *Al Monitor.* Accessed, Dec 11,2016. At: http://www.al-monitor.com/pulse/tr/originals/2014/02/isis-gaza-salafist-jihadist-qaeda-hamas.html#

Allawi, Ali. (2007), *The Occupation of Iraq,* New Haven, CT: Yale University Press.

Allen, John. (2015), Countering ISIS. *Brookings.* Accessed, October 14, 2017. At: http://www.brookings.edu/-/media/events/2015/06/01-2015-us-islamic-world-forum/060315brookingsdoha.pdf.

Alston, Philip. (2005), *Non-State Actors and Human Rights,* New York: Oxford University Press.

Al-Tamimi. (2014), Jamaat Ansar Bayt al-Maqdisi allegiance to Islamic State. *Pundicity.* Accessed, May 12, 2016. At:http://www.aymennjawad.org/2014/11/analysis-jamaat-ansar-bayat-al-maqdis-allegiance

Assaf, Moghadam, The salafi Jihad as a Religious Ideology, *CTC Sentinel 1,* no.3. Accessed, February 2017, at: http://www.ctc.usma.edu/posts/the-salafi-jihad-as-a-religious-ideology.

Ataman, Muhittin. (2003), The impact of Non-State Actors on world politics. *Turkish Journal of International Relations,* Vol.2, No.1

Aydinli, Ersel. (2016), *Violent Non-State Actors: from Anarchist to jihadist,* Britain: Routledge.

Banks, Michael. (1984), *Conflict in World Society: A New Perspective on International Relations,* New York: St. Martin's Press.

Barbara, Starr. (2016), Army Delta Force Begins to Target ISIS in Iraq. *CNN.* Accessed, November 26, 2017. At: http://www.cnn.com/2016/02/29/politics/pentagon-army-targets-isis-iraq/

Bayat, Asef. (2003), The Street and the politics of Dissent in the Arab World. *Middle East Report,* No.226, pp.10-17.

Bayat, Asef. (2007), *Making Islam Democratic: Social Movements and the Post-Islamist Turn,* Stanford: Stanford University Press.

Belfiore, Michael. (2010), *Islam in the Middle Ages,* U.S.A : Abcoclio.

Bellin, Eva. (2008), New Trends in the Study of Religion and Politics. *World Politics.* Vol. 60, no.2. pp 315–319.

Berger J.M, Stern Jessica. (2015), *ISIS: The State Of Terror,* Great Britain:William Collins.

Blin, Arnauld. (2011), Armed Groups and Intra State Conflicts: The Dawn of a New Era. *International Review of the Red Cross* 93, no.882: 287–310.

Brekke, Torkel. (2012), *Fundamentalism: Prophesy and Protest in the Age of Globalisation.* New York: Cambridge University Press.

Bremmer, Ian. (2015), The New Caliphate. *Time.* March 30, p 8.

Brisard, Jean. (2005), *Zarqawi: The New Face of Al-Qaeda,* New York: Cambridge Polity Press.

Brown, S. (1995), *New Forces, Old Forces, and the Future of World Politics,* New York: Harper Collins College Publishers.

Bull, Hedley. (1977), *The Anarchical Society: A Study of Order in world politics,* New York: Columbia University Press.

Cavanaugh.W, Hasler. K, Hassner. R, Inboden. W, Omer. A, Rosato. S, Saiya. N, Shah. T, Snyder. J, Toft. M and Verdeja. E. (2012), *Religion and International Relations,* New York: University of Notre Dame Press.

Cherain, John. (2015), Agents of Death. *Frontline.* December 11, pp 10–14.

Christopher Blanchard, Carla Humud, Kenneth Katzman and Matthew Weed. (2015), *The Islamic State Crisis and US policy*, U.S.A.: Congressional Research Service.

Clark, C. and Chan, S. (1995), MNCs and Developmentalism: Domestic Structure as an Explanation for East Asian Dynamism. In, Thomas Risse Kappen, ed. *Bringing Transnational Relations Back In: Non-State Actors, Domestic Structures and International Institutions*, Cambridge: Cambridge University Press, pp. 112–145.

Cockburn, Patrick. (2015), *The Rise of Islamic State,* New Delhi: Leftword Books.

Congressional Research Service. (2013), *Mexico's Drug Trafficking Organisation: Source and Scope of the Violence,* U.S.A.

Connolly, Amanda. (2015), Canadian fighters killed in Syria pose paperwork problem for government families, *iPolitics.* Accessed, Dec 12, 2017. At: http://ipolitics.ca/2015/12/09/canadian-fighters-killed-in-syria-pose-paperwork-problem-for-government-families/

Craig, Khan. (2015), Pakistani Taliban Leaders pledge Alliance to Islamic State. *Washington Post.* Accessed, Dec 9, 2016. At: http://www.washingtonpost.com/world/pakistan-taliban-leaders-pledge-allaince-to-islamic-state/2014/10/14/34837e7e53df-11e4-809b-8cc0a295c773_story.html

Cronin, Audrey. (2015), ISIS is not a Terrorist Group. *Foreign Affairs.* March/April, pp 38–52.

Cronk, Terri. (2016), Counter ISIS Defence Ministers Unanimously Supports Objectives. *DOD News.* Accessed, September, 3, 2017. At: http://www.defense.gov/News-Article-

View/Article/655155/carter-counter-isil-defence-ministers-unanimously-support-objectives

Cunningham Eric, Deyoung Karen. (2016), Strikes from Iranian Air Base Shows Russia's Expanding Footprint in the Middle East. *The Washington Post.* Accessed, November 28, 2017. At: http://www.washingtonpost.com/world/russia-uses-iranian-air-base-to-bomb-syria/2016/08/16/6b2a30e2-6393-11e6-96c0-37533479f3f5_story.html.

Dalacoura, Katerina. (1998), *Islam, liberalism and Human Rights: Implications for International Relations,* London: I.B Tauris.

Dalacoura, Katerina. (2001), Islamist Movements as Non-State Actors and their Relevance to International Relations. In *Non-State Actors in world politics,* eds Wallace William and Josselin. New York: Palgrave.

Dalacoura, Katerina. (2011), *Islamist Terrorism and Democracy in the Middle East,* U.S.A.: Cambridge University Press.

Danahar, Paul. (2013), *The New Middle East,* London: Bloomsbury.

Daphne Josselin, Wallace William. (2001), *Non-State Actors in world politics,* New York: Palgrave.

David Kirkpatrick. (2017), ISIS harsh Brand on Islam is Rooted in Austere Saudi Creed. *New York Times.* Accessed, September 24, 2017. At: http://www.nytimes.com/2014/09/25/world/middleeast/isis-abu-bakr-baghdadi-caliph-wahhabi.html?_r=0

Democratic Control of Armed Forces and Geneva Call. (2015), *Armed Non-State Actors: Current Trends And Future Challenges.* Switzerland: Democratic Control of Armed Forces and Geneva Call.

Dhiman, S.C.(2015), *ISIS: Reconciliation, Democracy and Terror*, New Delhi: Neha Publishers.

Di Giovanni, Janine Leah Mcgrath Goodman and Damien Sharkov. (2014), How does ISIS fund its reign of terror. *Newsweek*. Accessed, April 7, 2017. At: http://www.newsweek.com/2014/11/14/how-does-isis-fund-its-reign-terror-282607.html

Dorian, Gieger. (2015), This is How ISIS Uses Social Media to Recruit American Teens. *Teen Vogue*, November 20, pp 8–9.

Dornan, R. (2011), Realists and Constructivists approaches to Anarchy. Accessed, December 12, 2017. At: http://www.e-ir.info/2011/08/29/realist-and-constructivist-approaches-to-anarchy/

Drumberg, Daniel. (2002), The trap of liberalised autocracy: Democratisation in the Arab World, *Journal of Democracy*, Vol.13, No.4, pp. 56–68.

Edwards, Beverley. (2013), *Islamic Fundamentalism since 1945*, Canada: Routledge.

Erelle, Anna. (2015), *In the Skin of a jihadist: Inside Islamic State's Recruitment Networks*, Great Britain: Harper Collins.

Esposito, John. (1992), The Islamic Threat, New York: Oxford University Press. quoted in, Hurd, Elizabeth. 2008. *The Politics of Secularism in International Relations*. New Jersey: Princeton University Press. p 29.

Fidler, John. (2008), Theory of Open Source Anarchy. *Indiana Journal of Global Legal Studies*, Vol.15, No.1, 259–284.

Fishman, Brian. (2008), Bombers, bank accounts and bleed out: Al-Qaeda's Road in and out of Iraq. *Combating Terrorism at West Point*. July 14.

Florini, A. (2000), *The Third Force: The Rise of Transnational Civil Society*, Washington DC: Brookings Institution.

Fox, Jonathan. (2001), Religion as an Overlooked Element in International Relations. *International Studies Review.* Vol. 3, no. 3, pp 53–64.

George, D. (1996), *Pax Islamica,* In Sidahmed.A, Ehteshami.A.(eds). *Islamic Fundamentalism.* Oxford: Westview Press.

Gerhom, Gorenberg. (2009), Settling for radicalism. *The Prospect.* Accessed, November 12, 2017. At: http://prospect.org/article/settling-radicalism

Ghosh, Bobby. (2006), An eye for an eye, *Time.* February 26.

Grogenberg, Gershom. (2009), Settling for Radicalism. *The Prospect.* Accessed, November 18, 2017. At: http://prospect.org/article/settling-radicalism

Harress, Christopher. (2014), ISIS Weapons Growing in Number, Sophistication: A Soviet, Balkan and American Mix, but The Group cant Use All Of Them. *International Business Times.* Accessed, May 2, 2017. At: http://www.ibtimes.com/isis-weapons-growing-number-sophistication-soviet-balkan-american-mix-group-cant-use-all-1659176

Hassan, G. (2015), Libyan gains may offer ISIS a base for new attacks. *Washington Post.* Accessed, Jan 13, 2016. At: http://www.washingtonpost.com/world/middle_east/in-libyas-civil-war-the-islamic-state-shows-itself-as-the-main-threat/2015/06/06/65766592-0879-11e5951e-8e15090d64ae_story.html

Hayajneh, Adnan. (2004), The U.S Strategy: Democracy and Internal Stability in the Arab World. *Turkish Journal of International Relations,* Vol.3, No.2&3, p.25.

Heloise, Ruaudel. (2013), *Armed Non-State Actors and Displacement in Armed Conflicts,* Switzerland: Geneva Call.

Hendawi, Hamza and Zahra. (2015), ISIS is making up to $50 million a month from oil sales. *Business Insider.* Accessed, Nov 26, 2016. At: http://www.businessinsider.com/isis-making-50-million-a-month-from-oil-sales-2015–10

Henry, Schuster. Al-Zarqawi and Al-Qaeda in Jordan. *CNN.* Accessed, November 12, 2016, at: http://www.cnn.com/2005/WORLD/meast/11/11/zarqawi.jordan/index.html? =PM:WORLD

Holsti, Kalevi. (1996), *The State, War, and The State of War,* Cambridge: Cambridge University Press.

Hosken, Andrew. (2015), *Empire of Fear: Inside the Islamic State,* U.K.: One World.

Human Rights Watch. (2017), *World Report of 2017.* Accessed, December 22, 2017. At: https://www.hrw.org/sites/default/files/world_report_download/wr2017-web.pdf

Huntington, Samuel. (1991), *The third wave: Democratisation in the late twentieth century,* U.S.A.: Oklahoma Press.

Huntington, Samuel. (1997), *Clash of Civilisations And The Remaking Of world order,* Gurgaon: Penguin Books.

Ibrahim, Saad. (1998), The Troubled Triangle: Populism, Islam and Civil Society in the Arab World. *International Political Science Review.* Vol.19, No.4, pp 18-36.

Issacharoff, R. (2015), Gazans nabbed in Sinai Were Hamas Naval Commandos en Route to Training. *Times of Israel.* Accessed, March 18, 2017. At: http://www.timesofisrael.com?gazans-nabbed-in-sinai-were-hamas-naval-commandos-enroute-to-training/?utm_source=dlvr, it&utm_medium=Twitter

Jan. H Pierskalla, Florian M. Hollenbach. (2013), Technology and Collective Action: The effect of Cell Phone Coverage on Political Violence in Africa. *American Political Science Review* 107, no. 2. 2013. Pp 207-20.

Jane, Arraf. (2016), Islamic State Persecution of Yazidi minority amounts to genocide, UN says. *Christian Science Monitor.* Accessed, September 17, 2016. At: http://www.csmonitor.com/World/Middle-East/2014/0807/Islamic-State-persecution-of-yazidi-minority-amounts-to-genocide-UN-says

Jeremy, Sharp. (2015), Yemen: Civil War and Regional Intervention. *Congressional Research Service.* Accessed, Dec 1, 2016. At: https://www.fas.org/sgp/crs/mideast/R43960.pdf

Jeremy, J. (2015), Boko Harem's roots in Nigeria long predate Al-Qaeda era. *AlJazeera.* Accessed Oct. 10, 2017. At: http://america.aljazeera.com/articles/2014/4/23/boko-harem-s-rootsinnigerialongpredatethealqaedaera.html

John, F. (2014), Special Presidential Envoy for the Global Coalition to Counter ISIL. *Brookings.* Accessed, November 25, 2017. At: http://www.brookings.edu/-/media/events/2015/06/01-2015-us-islamic-world-forum/060315brookingsdoha.pdf

Johny, Stanley. (2015), Understanding and countering IS. *The Hindu,* July 8.

Johny, Stanley. (2015), Where does IS get money from? *The Hindu*, November 24.

Joscelyn, B. (2015), New Leader of Islamic Caucasus Killed by Russian Forces. *Long War Journal.* Accessed, Dec. 10, 2016. At: http://www.longwarjournal.org/archives/2015/08/new-leader-of-islamic-caucasus-emirate-killed-by-russian-forces.php

Kamrava, Mehran. (2005), *The Modern Middle East: A political history since the First World War.* London: University of California.

Kaviraj Sudipa, Khilani Sunil. (2001), *Civil Society: History and Possibilities.* U.S.A.: Cambridge University Press.

Kazimi, Nibras. (2015), Al-Baghdadi Name Pseudonyms – for Ministerial Portfolios. *Talisman Gate Blog.* Accessed, April 28, 2017. At: http://talismangate.blogspot.co.uk/2007/04/Al-Baghdadi-names-pseudonymsfor.html

Kazleh, A. (2006), Rethinking International Relations Theory in Islam: Towards a More Adequate Approach. *Turkish Journal of International Relations.* Vol.5, no. 4, pp 41-56.

Kenner, David. (2015), The Men Who Love The Islamic State. *Foreign Policy.* Accessed, September. 10, 2017. At: http://foreignpolicy.com/2015/02/04/islamic-state-jordan-zarqa/

Knickmeyer, Ellen. (2010), Blood on our hands, *Foreign Policy,* October 25.

Lamont, Christopher. (2015), *Research Methods in IR,* London: Sage.

Lander, Mark. (2017), Trump takes the greatest risk of his young presidency. *The Hindu.* April 8.

Latin, David. (1978), Religion, Political Culture, and the Weberian Tradition. *World Politics.* Vol. 30, no. 4, p 570.

Lekas, Annalise. (2015), ISIS: The Largest Threat to the World Peace. Accessed, October 3, 2017. At: http://law.emory.edu/eilr/content/volume-30/issue-2/comment/isis-largest-threat-world-peace.html

Lister, Charles. (2015), *The Islamic State,* India: Harper Collins.

Locks, Tim. (2016), *Fighting ISIS: How one ordinary Brit went to a War,* London:Sidgwick & Jackson.

Lutz James, lutz Brenda. (2013), *Global Terrorism,* U.S.A.: Routledge.

Mahmood, Mona. (2015), Double-layered veils and despair… women describe life under ISIS. *Guardian.* Accessed, March 3, 2017. At: http://www.theguardian.com/world/2015/feb/17/isis-orders-women-iraq-syria-veils-gloves

Masoud, Zackie (trans). (2013), An analysis of Abu Mus'ab al-Suri's Call to Global Islamic Resistance. *Journal of Strategic Security.* Vol 6, no.1, pp 1-18.

Mcinnis, Kathleen J. (2016), *Coalition contribution to countering the Islamic State,* U.S.A.: Congressional Research Service.

Menon, Parvathi. (2015), Unaccompanied refugees on the rise in Europe: OECD. *The Hindu.* September 23.

Mia, Bloom. (2014), How the Islamic State Is recruiting Western Teen Girls. *Washington Post.* Accessed, December 18, 2017. At:http://www.washingtonpost.com

Moon, Cronk. (2016), Counter ISIS support objectives. Accessed, November 26, 2017. At: http://www.defense.gov/News-Article-View/Article?655155/carter-counter-isil-defence-ministers-unanimously-support-objectives

Mueller, John. (1989), *Retreat from Doomsday: The Obsolescence of Major War,* New York: Basic Books.

Mukhopadhyay, Sounak. (2015), Russian militants pledge alliance to ISIS. *International Business Times*. Accessed Feb. 10, 2017. At: http://www, ibtimes.com/russian-militants-pledge-alliance-isis-forces-1981975

Naji, Tawhish. (2006), Management of the Savagery, (trans) William McCants. John M. Olin. *Institute for Strategic Studies*. U.S.A.: Harvard University Press.

Nance, Malcolm. (2016), *Defeating ISIS*, New York: Skyhorse Publishers.

Nasr, Seyyed. (2004), *The Heart of Islam*, U.S.A : Harper Collins Publisher.

Nawaf. S. (2014), The Saudis can crush ISIS. *New York Times*. Accessed, Oct 8, 2017. At: http://www.nytimes.com/2014/11/14/us-mideast-crisis-baghdadi-id-idUSKCN01X1Y12014114#DbDUkeWcODVZI1JQ.97

Nazish, Kiran. (2014), Islamic State is Spreading into Pakistan. *New Republic*. Accessed, Dec 9, 2016. At: http://newrepublic.com/article/119535/isis-pakistan-islamic-state-distributing-flags-and-flyers

Pamela, Engel. (2015), These Toyota Trucks are popular with terrorists-here's why. *Business Insider.* Accessed, July 7, 2017. At: http://www.businessinsider.com/why-isis-uses-toyota-trucks-2015–10

Parish, Brent. (2014), The Growing ISIS Arsenal pt.1. *The Right Planet.* Accessed, March 14, 2017. At: http://www.therightplanet.com/2014/08/the-growing-isis-arsenal-pt-1/

Paul, Robertson. (2014), ISIS comes to Libya. *CNN*. Accessed, Jan 13, 2017. At: http://www.cnn.com/2014/11/18/world/isis-libya/

Peritz Aki, Rosenbach Eric. (2012), *Find, Fix, Finish: Inside the Counter-terrorism Campaigns That Killed Bin Laden and Devastated Al-Qaeda,* New York: Public Affairs.

Perry Marvin, Negrin Howard. (2008), *Theory and practice of Islamic Terrorism.* U.S.A: Palgrave Macmillan.

Philpott, Daniel. (2009), Has the Study of Global politics found Religion? *Annual Review of Political Science.* Vol. 12, pp 180–187.

Pollack, Kenneth. (2014), An Army to Defeat Assad. *Foreign Affairs,* September/October.

Prashad, Vijay. (2017), Turkey feels more and more socially divided, and erdogan may not govern to unity. *The Hindu,* April 19.

Proctor, H. (1965), *Islam in IR.* New York: Praeger.

Reuter, Christoph. (2015), The Terror Strategist: Secret Files Reveal the Structure of Islamic State, *SpiegelOnline International.* Accessed, July 29, 2016. At: http://www.spiegel.de/international/world/islamic-state-files--show-structure-of-islamist-terror-group-a-1029274.html

Ricks, Thomas. (2006), *Fiasco: The American Military Adventure in Iraq,* London: Allen Lane.

Rukmini, S. (2015), ISIS and the lonely young American. *The New York Times.* June 27.

Ruthven, Malise. (2012), *Islam: a very short introduction,* Great Britain: Oxford University Press.

Samir, Amin. (2012), *The People's Spring: The Future of Arab Revolution,* Cape Town: Pambazuka Press.

Saul, Heather. ISIS publishes penal code listing amputation, crucifixion, and stoning as punishments-and vows to vigilantly enforce it. *Independent.* Accessed, Dec 15, 2016. At: http://www.independent.co.uk/news/world/middle-east/isis-publishes-penal-code-lising-amputation-crucifixion-and-stoning-as-punishments-and-vows-to-9994878.html

Schmitt, Carl. (1985), *Political Theology: Concept of Sovereignty,* (trans). Schwab, George. Chicago: University of Chicago Press. p 36.

Schneckener, Claudia. (2011), Engaging Non-State Armed Actors in State and Peace Building: Options and Strategies. *International Review of the Red Cross 93, no 883,* pp *603–621.*

Scott, Richard, Andrew, Matthew, Christian and Jacqui True. (2001), *Theories of International Relations.* New York: Palgrave.

Sekulow, Jay. (2014), *Rise of ISIS: A threat we cannot ignore,* New York: Howard.

Seth, Jones. (2015), Expanding the Caliphate. *Foreign Affairs.* Accessed, Feb 13, 2017. At: http://www.foreignaffairs.com/articles/afghanistan/2015-06-11/expanding-caliphate

Shadid, Anthony. (2010), Church Attack seen as Strike at Iraq's core. *New York Times.*November 1.

Shankar, S. (2014), Algerian Army kills Leader of Jund al-Khilafa Group That Beheaded French Tourist Herve Gourdel:Report. *International Business Times.*Accessed, October 13, 2017. At: http://www.ibtimes.com/algerian-army-kills-leader-jund-al-khilafa-group-beheaded-french-tourist-herve-1765668

Shaw, Malcolm. (2008), *International Law.* Cambridge University Press.

Shaw, Mark and Mangan. (2014), Illicit Trafficking and Libya's Transition. *United States Institute of Peace.* Accessed Jan 13,

2017. At: http://www.usip.org/sites/default/files/PW96-illicit-Trafficking-and-Libyas-Transition.pdf

Siman, Adams. (2015), *Failure to Protect: Syria and the UN Security Council*, New York: Global Centre for Responsibility to Protect.

Simpson Cam, Matthew Philips. (2015), Why US Efforts to Cut Off Islamic State's Funds Have Failed. *Bloomberg*. Accessed, August 13, 2017. At: http://www.bloomberg.com/news/articles/2015-11-19/why-u-s-efforts-to-cut-off-islamic-state-s-funds-have-failed

Singh, Ningthoujam. (2013), *Non-Traditional Security in International Relations*, India: Ruby Press & Co.

Singh, Ningthoujam. (2016), Non-Traditional Security: Redefining State-Centric Outlook. *Jadavpur Journal of International Relations*. 20(1), pp 102-124.

Sissions, S and al-Saiedi, A. (2013), A Bitter Legacy of De-Ba'athification in Iraq. *International Centre for Transnational Justice*. March 14, p 4.

Smith and Mills. (2015), *Iraq and Syria update 2015*, U.K: House of Commons.

Smith, Ben and Claire. (2017), Syria and Iraq Update. *House of Commons*. Accessed, December 28 2017. At: http://www.parliament.uk/commons-library

Smith, Grant, Ilya Arkhipov, and Henry Meyer. (2015), Obama and Putin agree on Bombing Islamic State's Oil Pipeline. *Bloomberg*. Accessed, September 13, 2017. At: http://www.bloomberg.com/news/articles/2015-11-19/obama-in-sync-with putin-on-bombing-islamic-state-oil-riches

Smith. (2016), *Iraq and Syria update 2016*. U.K: House of Commons.

Sood, Rakesh. (2015), Winds of change in West Asia. *The Hindu.* July 27.

Stakelbeck, Eric. (2015), *ISIS Exposed: beheadings, slavery and the hellish reality of Radical Islam,* U.S.A: Regnery.

Stent, Angela. (2016), Putin's Power Play in Syria. *Foreign Affairs.* January/February 2016, pp 106-109.

Stern, Jessica. (2003), *Terror in the name of God: Why Religious Militants Kill,* New York: Ecco.

The Brief. (2015), France's Assimilation Policy. November 30-December 7. p 27.

The Brief. (2015), Why The World Cries For The City Of Light. Nov 30-Dec 7. P 39.

The Economist. (2015), Awkward Allies, August 1. pp 39–40.

The Economist. (2015), Divided Country, Divided Narratives. July 11, p 70.

The Economist. (2015), Islamic State: The propaganda war. August.

The Economist. (2017), Chemical weapons in Syria. April, pp 38–39.

The Economist. (2017), Defeating Islamic State: Caliphate at Bay. March, pp 39–40.

The Economist. (2017), Gaza: Hamas Divided. April, p 40.

The Economist. (2017), Iran: Rouhani Under Fire. May. Pp 35–36.

The Economist. (2017), Islam in Indonesia: the rise of intolerance. April. 9.

The Economist. (2017), Jihadist in Bangladesh. April, p 23.

The Economist. (2017), Mine strategy. April, p 39.

The Economist. (2017), Saudi Arabia: The smell of burnt rubber. April, pp 34–35.

The Economist. (2017), Syria: Truncheons at a gunfight. March, p 38.

The Economist. (2017), Syria: What next? April, p 10.

The Economist. (2017), Terror and counter-terror. April, p 39.

The Economist. (2017), The battle for Mosul: going west. Feb, pp 37–38.

The Economist. (2017), The race for Raqqa. March, pp 40–41.

The Economist. (2017), Turkey:Judgement Day. May, pp 37–38.

The Economist. (2017), Who runs Iraq? April, pp 39–40.

The Economist. (2017), Yemen: Atomised. April, pp 35–36.

The Economist. (2015), The Fortunes of War. May 30, pp 47–48.

The Economist. (2016), Wave after Wave: why migrants will keep coming. Jan 1, p 67.

The Frontline. (2015), Agents of Death. December 11. pp 10–15.

The Frontline.(2015), Domino Theory An Empirical Investigation: Terror in Paris. December 11.

The Hindu. (2017), IS claims responsibility for U.K attack. March 24.

The Hindu. (2017), A reckless intervention. April 10.

The Hindu. (2017), After Mosul. March 11.

The Hindu. (2017), IS leaders are fleeing Raqqa. March 10.

The Hindu. (2017), Mother of all bombs. April 15.

Theodore, J. (2015), In Jordan, ISIS Hits a Wall…for Now. *AL Arabiya News.* Accessed, July 10, 2017. At: http://english. alarabiya.net/en/views/news/middle-east/2014/06/30/Jordan-s-stand-ISIS-hits-a-wall-for-now.html

Thomson, Peter. (2014), *Armed Groups: The 21st Century Threat,* New York: Rowman & Littlefield.

Time.(2014), The Blowback. July.

Time. (2014), Threat Assessment. October 6.

Time. (2015), Putin's Syria Gamble. October 26.

Time. (2015), The New Caliphate. March 30, pp 8.

Time. (2017), The Trump Effect. March, pp 14–19.

Time. (2017), When the call comes. Feb, p 24.

Toft, Monica. (2012), *Religion and International Relations Theory,* Oxford: Oxford University Press.

Tripathi, D. The Roots Of Europe's Refugee Crisis. *The Hindu.* Accessed, January 8, 2016. At: http://www.thehindu. com/opinion/op-ed/the-roots-of-europes-refugee-crisis/article7648732.ece

Turner, John. (2012), Uncovering an Islamic Paradigm of International Relations. (eds). Flood, Christopher. In *Political and Cultural Representation of Muslims: Islam in the Plural.* New York: Brill.

United Nations High Commissioner or Refugees. (2016), Global Trends: Forced Displacement. Accessed, November 2, 2017. At: http://www.unhcr.org/statistics

United Nations Security Council. (2014), *Threats to International Peace and Security Caused By Terrorist Acts*. United Nations Security Council. S/PV.7272.

US Homeland Security Committee. (2015), Terror Threat Snapshot. Accessed, Dec 20, 2015. At: https://homeland.house.gov/wp-content/uploads/2015/12December-Terror-Threat-Snapshot.pdf

Valensi, Carmit. (2015), Non-State Actors: A theoretical Limitation on Changing Middle East. *Military and Strategic Affairs*. Volume7. No.1, pp 1–18.

Voskopoulos, George. (2015), The Arab Spring Phenomenon and European Security: Change and Continuity Under the Spectrum of Secularised Idealism. *The IUP Journal of International Relations, Vol.IX, No.3*, pp 22–34.

Wickramasinghe, A. (2015), *Islamic State and the Demise of Westphalia*, Sri Lanka: University of Colombo.

Wiktorowicz, Quintan. (2007), Civil Society and Social Control: State Power in Jordan. *Comparative Politics*. Vol.33, No.1, pp.43–61.

William, McCants, (trans). (2006), *Management of Savagery: The most critical stage through which the umma will pass*. U.S.A.: John M. Olin Institute for Strategic Studies at Harvard University.

Williams, Jennifer. (2015), The Saudi Arabia Problem: Why a country at war with jihadists also fuels them. *Vox*. Accessed, March 20, 2016. At: http://www.vox.com/2015/12/1/9821446/saudi-problem-isis

World Focus.(2004), The Iraq Crisis: An overview. Vol.25, No.1, pp 5–11.

Zeidan, David. (2001), Islamic Fundamentalist view of life as a perennial battle. *MERIA Journal*. June 2. Vol. 3. pp 26–53.

Zubaida, S. (1993), *Islam, the People and the State: Political Ideas and Movements in the Middle East.* London: I.B Tauris.